THE

JPMGUIDES

From the Black Forest to the Puszta

Who can hear the name Danube without thinking of that most famous of Strauss waltzes: "On the Beautiful Blue Danube"? Beautiful it certainly is, but to be honest, it's more a brownish yellow than blue, thanks to the lime stirred up from the river bed. The Danube's romance lies in the medieval castles, baroque churches and rococo palaces it passes on its way through central Europe and the Balkans.

The great waterway begins in southwest Germany at the confluence of the Brege and the Brigach, and flows on through eight other countries—Austria, Slovakia, Hungary, Croatia, Serbia, Romania, Bulgaria and Ukraine. Its 2,850 km (1,770 miles) make it Europe's second longest river, after the Volga. Barge traffic starts at the cathedral town of Ulm, larger vessels at Regensburg. Today, completion of the Main–Danube Canal extends navigation from the North Sea to the Black Sea delta, more than 3,200 km (2,000 miles).

The Danube crosses from Germany into Austria at Passau, established as a frontier town by the Romans. It flows through the major port town of Linz to the Habsburgs' grand imperial city of Vienna. From Slovakia's proud capital, Bratislava, the river follows the Hungarian border until it makes a 90° turn at the dramatic Danube Bend, crossing Hungary's Great Alföld Plain to golden Budapest, which proudly claims the title "Queen of the Danube". The river cleaves through the city, separating the old hill town of Buda from the more modern Pest. Beyond the residential and industrial suburbs—which go on and on, for the capital is ten times bigger than any other Hungarian town, the river returns to its bucolic mood, flowing through flat, fertile countryside concealing, more often than displaying, the traces of a dramatic history. In all, the Danube stretches 417 km (260 miles) through Hungary.

Whereas Budapest is proud of its bridges spanning the wide river (the first was built in 1849), the southern stretch is almost bridge-free. Ferries for cars and passengers thus play their traditional role. Otherwise, the river traffic ranges from cruise ships and freighters to tugboats and rowing boats.

Dürnstein is one of the most attractive little towns on the banks of the Danube.

Early times	One of the earliest cultures arises around 8000–7000 BC in Lepenski Vir, in modern-day Serbia, as attested by the discovery of carved stones. Trade along the Danube develops as early as the Neolithic. The original inhabitants of Bulgaria, the Thracians, spread to the lands between the lower Danube and the northern Aegean around 1000 BC.
1st century BC	From 27 BC, under Emperor Augustus, Roman conquest of the Danube Valley makes the river (*Danubius*, and in its lower reaches, the *Ister*) the empire's northern border against barbarians—Celts, Pannonians and Illyrians. Some 20,000 Roman soldiers are deployed along the river between Vienna and Budapest. Frontier outposts are established at Castra Regina (Regensburg), Castra Batava (Passau), Lentia (Linz), Vindobona (Vienna), Posonium (Bratislava) and Aquincum (Budapest).
4th–9th centuries AD	From the 4th century, the Danube plain is overrun by fearsome hordes of Goths, Attila's Huns and Avars from the Asian steppes. Emperor Charlemagne drives them out in the 8th century, but they are followed by Magyars settling in Hungary from somewhere between the Volga river and the Ural mountains, along with a few Turkic Pechenegs and Curmans.
10th–14th centuries	Hungary's conversion to Christianity in 975 makes the Danube a safe overland route for pilgrims going to the Holy Land. The river proves rather more perilous when French and German Crusaders choose it in 1096 for their pillaging progress through Austria and Hungary to "save" Constantinople and Jerusalem from Islam. England's Richard I the Lion-Heart is imprisoned in Dürnstein Castle on his way home from Palestine in 1192. In 1396, an army of 100,000 Germans, French, Hungarians, Poles, Bohemians, Italians and Spaniards congregates at Budapest and advances down the Danube—to meet crushing defeat by the Turks at Nicopolis, now Nikopol in Bulgaria.
16th–18th centuries	In the 16th century, the Danube becomes the route of a "crusade" in reverse, as Suleiman the Magnificent's Ottoman Turks carry Islam west from the Black Sea.

They defeat the Hungarians at Mohács in 1526 and three years later advance to the walls of Vienna. Forced to retreat, the Ottoman forces content themselves with capturing Budapest in 1541. They hold the city for the next 150 years. A second siege of Vienna is repelled in 1683, but the Turks continue to control the lower Danube.

After the Hungarian rulers move their capital to Bratislava, the Austrian Habsburgs inherit the heart of the Danube valley to the west. Maria Theresa, crowned "King of Hungary" brings stability in the 18th century, The Habsburgs give the region its many elegant baroque and rococo monuments—including Vienna's Schönbrunn Palace, Melk abbey and Krems parish church. Vienna is swept by regular floods, despite efforts to harness its waters, beginning with the Danube Canal built in 1598.

19th century

In 1856, after the Crimean War, the river's first navigation commission is established to ease German and Austrian eastbound traffic by clearing the Black Sea delta of its debris. Ten years later, a more romantic note is struck by Johann Strauss composing his Blue Danube waltz. In the 1870s, to combat flooding, the Danube is diverted around the city of Vienna.

20th century

After World War I the Austro-Hungarian Monarchy collapses (1918); the Danube lands become independent states. In 1932 a conference on Danubian affairs is held in London. The French prime minister Tardieu suggests unification of the Danubian region (excepting Germany and Italy), but his plan falls through. In World War II, the Danube becomes a front line. German naval forces use the river to reach the Black Sea. The victorious Soviet army occupies Budapest, Belgrade, Transylvania, Walachia and the Banat in 1944, and introduces a Communist regime. With this move, the USSR achieves supremacy in the Danubian region and the Balkans.

The fall of the Berlin Wall in 1989 and the breakup of former Yugoslavia into independent republics has far-reaching consequences for all the states on the middle and lower Danube.

Distances on the Danube are measured in kilometres starting at Sulina on the delta, km 0.

Along the River

At its crossing point from Germany into Austria, the Danube is joined by two other rivers, the sturdy Inn from the south and the little Ilz from the north. Champions of the Inn (which gives its name to Innsbruck) note that it is broader and bluer here than the Danube, and so much more deserving of Johann Strauss's waltz.

Passau (km 2227), the town that straddles the confluence of the three rivers, is a solid old bishopric that has always enjoyed the good life, celebrating its religious festivities with plenty of music, beer for the men and hot chocolate for the ladies. Historically prospering from the trades in wine, wheat and salt, it is an inviting city, from the bulbous onion domes and graceful arches of its baroque monuments to the rounded promontories separating the waterways. For a fine view over the town's charming backdrop of green wooded hillsides, make your way up to the Oberhaus fortress. The castle museum offers a good introduction to the region's art and craftwork—of old, Passau rivalled Damascus and Toledo for the delicate workmanship of its finely honed sword blades. Exhibits also trace the history of shipping on the Danube.

Over to the south, the core of the town stands on the ridge of land between the Danube and

6

Inn rivers. Towering over it is the cathedral of St Stephan, with its three onion domes, Flamboyant Gothic chancel, rich baroque interior boasting a total of 1,000 sculpted figures, and the world's biggest church organ, with 17,774 pipes.

Standing where the valley flattens into a plain, on a major crossroads to Germany and the Czech Republic, **Linz** (km 2135) is capital of the province of Upper Austria and centre of the country's heavy industry. Back in 1832, it was the starting point of Austria's first "railway"—with horses providing the locomotive power, pulling wagons to Budweis in Bohemia. Five years later, the first steamship moored here. Today, the huge VOEST steel plant is located across the Nibelung Bridge on the north bank, along with important chemical factories. The port, separated from the river by a protective harbour with special wharves, is Austria's biggest, handling 5 million tonnes of goods per year.

The old city is nicely preserved on the south bank, cen-

PASSAU'S PACIFISTS

The people of Passau have always been far too fond of the good life to spoil it by wasting time fighting. When the town was besieged by the Bavarians in 1703, the bishop's three companies of soldiers declined to report for duty, explaining that they had all come down with a fever. The Bavarian forces were eventually able to complete their conquest, but not until 1741—and their general, much frustrated, complained that he had met no opposition at all!

7

tred around a main square (Hauptplatz) surrounded by handsome houses of the 17th and 18th centuries and an imposing Gothic Rathaus (town hall). In the centre of the square is the tall, twisting Dreifaltigkeitssäule (Trinity Pillar), set up in 1723 to commemorate the town's deliverance from ten years of war, fire and plague. The square's grand baroque Jesuitenkirche is known locally as the "old cathedral", having served as such till 1909. Its façade is graced by statues of three Jesuit heroes, Ignatius Loyola, Francis Xavier and Francis Borgia (a rare saintly figure in that notorious family). It was here that Anton Bruckner (1824–96) played the organ. The oldest church in town, perhaps in all Austria, is Martin-

8 skirche on Römerstrasse, dating

back at least to Emperor Charlemagne in 799. The 16th-century seat of government on Klosterstrasse, the Landhaus, is a gracious Renaissance building, notable for the flower-bedecked balconies of its arcaded courtyard. The provincial museum, housed in the remains of the old castle, is devoted to local history and exhibitions of modern

ADOPTIVE SONS

If it prefers to forget that Adolf Hitler spent several years of his youth in Linz (and dreamt of ending his days here), the town is proud to celebrate the great 17th-century astronomer Johannes Kepler, who taught at the university, and 19th-century composer Anton Bruckner, the town's organist. It also has links with Mozart who created his *Linzer Symphonie* here in 1783.

art. For a good view of the surrounding countryside and the Alps, an electric railway makes the steep climb to the top of the Pöstlingberg over on the north bank.

Mauthausen (km 2112), originally established as an imperial customs station at the confluence with the Enns river, is now more bitterly remembered as the site of Austria's largest concentration camp. A chapel and a monument commemorate its 100,000 victims. The stone quarries where slave labour cut granite for Vienna's building material are now the setting for an international sculpture symposium.

One of the most romantic stretches of the Danube is the **Wachau**, winding its way just 30 km (19 miles) between Melk and Krems. Friendly country villages flanked with apricot orchards and vineyards alternate with dark castle ruins on craggy cliffs. Some of Austria's best white wines and potent *Marillenbrand* (apricot brandy) are nurtured here, along with the passionate, murderous legends of the Nibelungs that inspired Richard Wagner's operas.

The handsome castle of Greinburg watches over the little town of **Grein** (km 2079), which has a lovely rococo theatre in the main square, unaltered since it was built in 1790.

Long before **Melk** (km 2036) became the home of the Benedictines in 1089, its clifftop position above the river bend made it an ideal military camp from which to fend off barbarians. Elegant as it now is, the 18th-century abbey you see today still looks a lot like a 9

fortress, built where the Babenbergs had previously sited their own palace stronghold. In 1702, architect Jakob Prandtauer was commissioned to transform the forbidding strategic fortification

into a splendid baroque sanctuary with gracefully tapering towers and a majestic octagonal dome.

Dürnstein (km 2009) is famous above all for the medieval dungeon where Richard I the Lion-Heart was held prisoner on his return from the Crusades. It cost England 23,000 kg of silver to secure his release. In 1645, during the Thirty Years' War, the Swedes left the hillside castle in ruins. Be sure to visit the town's cheerful baroque abbey church.

Krems (km 2002), the centre of the Wachau's wine industry, has retained an old-town charm. Gothic pepperpot towers greet you at the 15th-century Steiner Tor (city gate). Another Gothic masterpiece is the older Gozzo-Burg patrician residence on Hoher Markt, the town's oldest

ROYAL CHORUS

In 1191, Richard the Lion-Heart tried to sneak through the Danube Valley disguised as a peasant. At Acre in Palestine, the King of England had upset Duke Leopold V von Babenberg by raising the English banner in place of the Austrian and appropriating all the booty. He was recognized by the Austrians, apprehended and jailed in Dürnstein—where his faithful minstrel Blondel tracked him down by wandering along the river singing a popular English ballad until he heard the king joining in the chorus.

square. The museum housed in the old Dominikanerkirche displays the medieval art and history of Krems. The 17th-century Veitskirche (Church of St Vitus) is an attractive baroque edifice by Italian architects, with altar paintings by Franz Anton Maulpertsch and frescoes by Martin Johann ("Kremser") Schmidt. But for many, the most enjoyable monuments are the Renaissance houses on Obere Landstrasse, where they serve the new *Heuriger* wine in tree-shaded courtyards.

The Augustine abbey at **Klosterneuburg** (km 1939) was founded in 1114 and rebuilt by Emperor Karl VI in the 18th century to emulate the Escorial in Madrid, home of his Spanish Habsburg ancestors. His dream of a vast palace-cum-church

with nine domes, each graced with a Habsburg crown, had to stop short at one big dome, with the imperial crown, and one little one, with the crown of the Austrian archduke. The major attraction of the interior is the Leopold Chapel's superb 12th-century Verdun Altar with its 45 Biblical scenes painted in enamel panels. As in Krems, the other attraction is outside, in the wine gardens set amid the vineyards at the edge of the Wienerwald (Vienna Woods).

The population of **Vienna** (km 1929), Austria's capital, reflects the cosmopolitan mix of peoples once ruled by the Habsburg Empire: Hungarians, Germans, Czechs, Slovaks, Poles, Spaniards, Flemings and Italians—as a glance in the phone book will confirm. They have all made a contribution to the 11

city's architecture, music and painting, but also to the cuisine of its restaurants and celebrated cafés.

Even if you don't have tickets for a performance, take a look at the Staatsoper (opera house) which the Viennese could scarcely wait to rebuilt after the

---

FREUDIAN SYMBOL

Vienna is the city of Sigmund Freud. The home of the founder of psychoanalysis, Berggasse 19, is now a museum. The house from which he was forced to flee in 1938 has many of the doctor's original furnishings and letters, his walking stick, hats and leather bags. Before you read too much into his empty cigar-case, remember the great man's warning about excessive interpretation of phallic symbols: "Sometimes a cigar is just a cigar."

---

destruction of World War II, the Burgtheater (national theatre) or the magnificent concert halls of the Musikverein and Konzerthaus. So sacred are the performing arts in Vienna, that the atmosphere in the opera house and concert halls is as hallowed as in a Christian cathedral or a Buddhist temple. Not that the towering St Stephen's Cathedral is denied pride of place in the centre of town. Defying eight centuries of war and fire, it remains a grandiose Gothic monument that expresses the city's spirit with both exuberance and dignity. Inside, be sure to see Anton Pilgram's beautifully sculpted Gothic pulpit.

Around the cathedral are monuments large and small. Wolfgang Amadeus Mozart lived in the modest Figarohaus, Domgasse 5. Vienna's oldest

tavern, the Griechenbeisl at Fleischmarkt 11, was a popular haunt of Beethoven and Schubert. The imperial glories of the Habsburgs are housed in their vast Hofburg palace, with its Renaissance and baroque royal apartments, library, chapel and stables for the renowned Spanish Riding School.

Two great museums: the Kunsthistorisches, famous for its Breughels, Dürers and Titians; and the Belvedere Palace devoted mainly to Austrian art of the 19th and 20th centuries. Schönbrunn, the Habsburgs' summer palace, is worth a visit as much for its lovely gardens as for the sumptuous apartments.

To the south of Vienna lies **Gumpoldskirchen**, one of the region's most charming wine-growing villages, and home of the famous white wine of that name. Be sure to visit the 16th-century Rathaus, the Gothic church and characteristic local inns offering the new wine, the "Heuriger".

The Cistercian abbey of **Heiligenkreuz** was founded in the 12th century. Its arcaded courtyard had to be rebuilt after an attack by the Turks, but the Romanesque nave and the basilica's Gothic choir remained intact. The Plague Column (*Pestsäule*) in the courtyard and the skilfully carved choir stalls are by the baroque artist Giuliani. The cloister, with its red marble pillars, exudes peace and harmony.

Mayerling achieved its claim to fame through a tragic event: the 30-year-old Crown Prince Rudolf and the 17-year-old Hungarian countess Maria Vetsera committed suicide together in the hunting lodge—their relationship had been condemned as scandalous, and Rudolf had been officially refused a divorce. Emperor Franz Joself had a Carmelite convent built on the spot where the couple died, and Maria Vetsera was buried in the cemetery of Heiligenkreuz, while Rudolf was laid to rest in the family tomb in Vienna.

Capital of Slovakia, **Bratislava** (km 1868) commands a key position close to Austria and Hungary. The new Danube–Oder canal links it to trade with Poland and eastern Germany. Following the Turkish capture of Budapest, Bratislava was the capital-in-exile for Hungary's kings and archbishops from 1541 to 1784. Today, its textile, chemical, oil and metal industries are offset by pleasant forests, vineyards and farmland surrounding a handsome baroque city centre. Towering over the town is the royal castle dating back to the 9th century, rebuilt in the 13th, but now largely Renaissance in style. It houses the Slovak National Museum. Hungarian coronations were held in St Martin's Gothic cathedral. The baroque palaces and town hall date from the golden Habsburg era of Maria Theresa.

Esztergom (km 1718), some 150 km (93 miles) southeast of Bratislava, was Hungary's first capital and royal seat under the Árpád kings. King Stephen was born here around 970, and founded the cathedral in 1010. The monarchy moved out after the Mongol invasions of the 13th century, but the archbishops stayed on, taking over the royal residence as their own. Esztergom was to pay the price for its ecclesiastical importance in 1543, when it was destroyed by the Turks. The restoration needed was so considerable that the Church only moved back again in 1820. And despite its clergy facing brutal persecution by the Communist authorities in the 1950s and 60s, the city has remained the centre of Hungarian Catholicism throughout.

The gigantic neoclassical basilica that towers over the city skyline is on the site of King Stephen's original cathedral. Begun in 1822, it took nearly 40 years to complete. The massive dome is based on St Peter's in Rome, and when it was finished, a consecration ceremony was held to the accompaniment of Liszt's specially composed *Gran Mass* ("Gran" being the German name for Esztergom).

The most outstanding feature of the voluminous interior is the Bakócz Chapel, built in red marble by Florentine Renaissance craftsmen in the early 16th century. It's the only part of the old cathedral left.

To the right of the main altar, the treasury contains a magnificent collection of textiles and medieval gold relics, including the 13th-century Coronation Cross used by Hungary's kings to pledge their oaths up to the last coronation—Charles IV—in 1916. In the crypt is the tomb of Cardinal Mindszenty. He opposed the Communist takeover after the war and was arrested and tortured. Released during the 1956 Uprising, he took refuge in the US Embassy for the next 15 years. He died in exile in 1975 and was reburied here with a state funeral in 1991.

You can complete your tour of the church by ascending the cupola for a superb view of both town and river. You'll need plenty of energy to tackle the last stage: a narrow, interminable spiral staircase, but it's well worth the effort.

The Castle Museum incorporates parts of the royal palace, including a 12th-century chapel and medieval Hall of Virtues, named after its frescoes depicting Moderation, Justice, Prudence and Fortitude.

Below the hill are the attractive baroque streets of the Viziváros, or Watertown. The Parish Church dates from 1738 and is in Italianate baroque style. In the old Primate's Palace, the Christian Museum houses what ranks as Hungary's greatest collection of religious art, with Italian prints, Renaissance paintings and the ornate 15th-century Garamszentbenedek coffin.

Beautiful green wooded hill country at a hairpin bend in the river just before the famous **Danube Bend** provides an idyllic setting for the remains of King Matthias Corvinus's opulent 15th-century palace at **Vise-**

HUNGARIAN CONNECTION

The legendary Count Dracula, who spread fear and trembling throughout Transylvania, was portrayed on screen by a Hungarian actor, Béla Lugosi. Other Hungarians who found fame and fortune in Hollywood are Peter Lorre, George Sanders, George Cukor, Michael Curtiz, Tony Curtis, Mitzi Gaynor and Zsa Zsa Gabor. Goldie Hawn and Drew Barrymore also have Hungarian origins.

grad (km 1695). Much of the sprawling residence—terraced into five levels on the hillside—has been restored. The monumental Hercules Fountain is a fine example of Hungarian Renaissance; the Court of Honour has graceful arcades.

Vác (km 1679) has a pretty baroque centre, its houses still painted green, red and ochre, compensating for the textile factories and cement works on the outskirts. The 18th-century cathedral boasts some remarkable frescoes by Franz Anton Maulpertsch, while the Triumphal Arch (1764) was purpose-built specially for a visit by Empress Maria Theresa.

Szentendre (km 1668) is a photogenic little town with a surprising quantity of art galleries and museums. Founded by Serbian refugees fleeing the Turks after the Battle of Kosovo in 1389, it received a second wave of Serbs three centuries later when the Turks recaptured Belgrade.

The main town square is the baroque Fő tér, with a votive cross put up by Serbian merchants in 1763 to celebrate the non-appearance of the plague. Here, too, is the green-spired Greek Orthodox Blagoveštenska Church, built ten years earlier. The icons inside are emphatically Serbian, however, and evoke the troubled history of that land.

Just behind the square's east side, an alley leads to the Margit Kovács Museum. Kovács, who died in 1977, created stylized, elongated sculptures from ceramics, and her work—part reinvention of religious iconic art, part folksy kitsch—is both striking and entertaining.

Leading south from Fő tér, Dumtsa Jeno utca has two excellent museums. The Barcsay Museum has architectural paintings, mosaics and tapestries by Transylvanian artist Jeno Barcsay. An altogether lighter confection can be enjoyed at the Marzipan Museum, where those with a sweet tooth can lick their lips over such items as a marzipan sculpture of the Parliament.

Until the 19th century, the Hungarian capital **Budapest** (km 1647) was two cities separated by the Danube, hilly Buda on the west bank and flat Pest to the feast. Each part has retained its character: Buda with its quiet streets around the splendid Matthias Church and the Royal Palace; Pest, the boisterous centre of the modern city.

All the towns along the Danube shores have their historic vestiges—perhaps a church built on the remains of a mosque, or the ruins of an ancient monastery. Even the prosaic industrial town **Dunaújváros** (km 1578), the "Danube New Town" constructed around a port and steel mills, has historical treasures to offer, with a park displaying ancient ruins and a museum dedicated to the Roman fortifications unearthed here.

The importance of **Dunaföldvár** (km 1561) is due to its road and rail bridge across the Danube. **Harta** (km 1546) on the left bank dates back to Swabian (German) settlers brought here by Austria's Empress Maria Theresa in the 18th century. Further downstream in **Paks** (km 1531) is to be found Hungary's one and only nuclear power station.

The farming town of **Kalocsa** (km 1515) has something for every taste—history, folklore,

art, and one of Europe's most offbeat museums. Kalocsa was founded in the 11th century alongside the Danube, but the river subsequently changed its mood and its course, leaving the town 6 km from the nearest fish or boat. Happily, the newly enlarged boundaries of Kalocsa included fertile meadows, where fruit and vegetables and grain grow. The dominant crop, though, is paprika. So it is that Kalocsa offers the Paprika Museum, where you can follow the saga of the Mexican hot pepper through its Hungarian naturalization. It didn't become an essential ingredient of the Hungarian diet until the early 19th century. One of the town's most photogenic features is the display, every autumn, of bright red peppers hanging to dry from the eaves of local houses. On a less romantic note, one of Ka-

HUNGARIAN WINES

Hungary will keep the most demanding wine-lover in a state of bliss. It's a huge producer of quality wines, though few are household names abroad. The renowned Tokaji (also spelt Tokay) as the jewel in its crown—the wine of kings and the king of wines. Made in the Tokaj region of the Northern Uplands, it uses native Furmint and Hárslevelü grapes and ranges from the pale, dry Tokaji Furmint to the rich amber Tokaji aszú dessert wine. The latter is one of the world's great sweet wines and has had its praises sung by Louis XIV, Beethoven, Schubert and Robert Browning—even Sherlock Holmes is known to have enjoyed the odd glass now and then. Its degree of sweetness is expressed in *puttonyos*, numbered from 3 to 6 (the sweetest) and indicating the quantity of baskets *(puttony)* of "noble" grapes added to each barrel of wine.

More popularly identified with Hungary is Bull's Blood from around Eger (Egri Bikavér), a red table wine whose name tells you all you need to know about its full-bodied character. It is a compound of four types of grapes. It goes perfectly with Hungary's abundance of meaty dishes, as do the younger reds, Kékfrankos and Kékoportó, and the fine Villányi-Burgundi.

But most of the country's wines are white. To accompany Lake Balaton fish, you should try a Lake Balaton wine. The Romans, who first brought wine-growing techniques to Hungary, loved the wines made here. From the vineyards around Badacsony, on the lake's north shore, look out for a range of white wines using well-known grape varieties, including the Olaszrízling, a medium-bodied Riesling, Traminer and Pinot Blanc.

locsa's principal employers is a giant paprika factory.

The Károly Viski Museum is one of the many folklore collections scattered around the country; in the case of Kalocsa there's no shortage of exhibits. The peasant costumes are a delight of floral designs—even the boys sport a splash of colour embroidered on their white shirts. Here, too, are displays of traditional farm tools, antique furniture and decorations.

The Kalocsa Folk Art Cooperative has its own museum, also devoted to antique agricultural implements and rustic home furnishings. Kalocsa embroidery is on show—and on sale—and they stage folklore exhibitions in which the local youngsters dance to typically vivacious Hungarian music.

Kalocsa's main square, Szabadság tér, features statues of two national heroes—King (Saint) Stephen and Franz Liszt. The 18th-century cathedral, in graceful baroque style, stands on the site of a series of churches, going back to the 11th century. In the Archbishop's Palace, across the square, the library contains more than 100,000 volumes, including a Bible autographed by Martin Luther.

The centre of a wine-growing region, the county seat of **Szekszárd**, more than 20 km (12

miles) from the river, has a high proportion of citizens of German and Serbian descent. Their pedigree can be traced back to the 150 years of Turkish occupation, when Szekszárd was a ghost town. To renew the population in the 18th century, settlers from neighbouring countries were welcomed. Local history starts in the 11th century, when King Béla I founded a fortified Benedictine monastery on a hill. The courtyard of the present County Hall is built around the remains of an ancient chapel and the abbey church.

If an invader wanted to split Hungary in half he could hardly do better than put out of commission the vulnerable Danube bridge at **Baja** (km 1479), the southernmost in Hungary. The vital link between east and west Hungary carries rail traffic as well as cars and trucks (eastbound and westbound alternate), all on a single lane. Long before there was a bridge, the Turkish invaders, aware of the strategic significance, fortified the town. Today the enormous main square, Béke tér, gives an idea of the historic importance of Baja.

A garden to wear: embroidered blouses are part of the traditional costume.

There are only two ways to visit the 14,000-ha (35,000-acre) game reserve of **Gemenc**, along both banks of the Danube near Baja: by boat or special narrow-gauge train. The area of forested moorland, crisscrossed by backwater loops of the river, is the home of deer, wild boar and a world of birdlife. Keen eyes may sight eagles, falcons, egrets or black storks. The reserve's Hunting Museum contains details of the region's fauna.

The Danube port city of **Mohács** (km 1448) is forever linked with a melancholy chapter in Hungarian history. It unfolded swiftly, a few kilometres out of town, on August 29, 1526. A well-equipped army of Sultan Suleiman the Magnificent, with a four-to-one advantage in manpower, crushed the defending forces of the Hungarian King Louis II. The king died during the retreat. For the next century and a half Hungary endured Ottoman occupation.

The modern Votive Church in the centre of town is one of the local memorials to these events. Meant to give thanks for the eventual expulsion of the Turks, it might be mistaken for a mosque, but the dome is topped by a big cross.

On the actual site of the 16th-century battle, a memorial park 21 is strewn with haunting modern sculptures symbolizing the opposing forces in the disastrous conflict. Here the ghosts of the generals, the soldiers and the horses—in imaginative woodcarvings—are forever deployed across the field of battle. The park was dedicated in 1976 on the 450th anniversary of an unforgettable defeat.

One way the people of Mohács celebrate the departure of the Turks is at Carnival time, when they parade in the scariest giant masks. The Busó carnival, the most spectacular folkloric manifestation in the country, also aims to expel another invader—winter.

The Hungarian version of the wild west—the puszta—conjures visions of gallant horsemen, lonely shepherds, pastures and dunes. It's all still there in **Kiskunság National Park**, 35,000 protected hectares (86,000 acres) of dramatic landscape between the Danube and the Tisza. Accomplished horsemen in baggy trousers and red waistcoats show the tourists their skills in a cross between a rodeo and a circus. Apart from the handsome horses there are herds of big-horned cattle and Racka sheep with screw-shaped horns. The birds that follow include red herons, great egrets and spoonbills.

One of the highlights of a visit to the puszta is a stop at a *czárda*, or wayside inn, where the food is as rustic as the surroundings. The meal is washed down with hearty Hungarian wine and music—including, perhaps, the wail of gypsy violins, or the spirited melodies of the *czárdás*.

SOAKING THE HUNGARIANS

You can't have everything. Hungary, occupying only one per cent of the area of Europe, lacks two significant geographical features: mountains to inspire skiers, and a seacoast. The landlocked country has to make do with the Danube and central Europe's biggest lake, Balaton. Bathing in Lake Balaton, which is rich in calcium and magnesium, is said to be good for you. The water is pleasantly warm, and your feet sink into the soft, sandy bottom, raising clouds of sand. It's certainly good for the fish: some of the pike-perch grow to 10 kg.

Any Hungarians not swimming in the Danube or Balaton are probably immersed in thermal baths. There are about 500 hot springs around the country, much appreciated since the time of the ancient Romans. Soaking in the spa waters—drinking them, too—is supposed to cure just about any ailment you can imagine.

THE WACHAU

Land of Vines and Apricots

"The Wachau" is the name given to the delightful stretch of the Danube between Melk and Krems in Lower Austria *(Niederösterreich)*. Just 30 km (19 miles) long, this belt of land basks in an exceptionally mild climate. Grapes and apricots *(Marillen* in Austrian German) flourish here, and the best way to enjoy them is to sample the delicious white wines, fiery apricot schnapps and rich abundance of cakes and desserts on offer in the local hostelries.

The name "Wachau" (formerly Wahowa) probably derived from *wacta* (watch-post on the river), or from the word *vahen,* to catch, as a reference to fishing.

Whatever your passion, the Wachau has something to offer: history buffs and adventurers can discover the castles from which robber barons used prey on merchant ships passing on the Danube; art lovers can marvel at the Benedictine abbey of Melk—a jewel of baroque architecture—and the lovely old town of Krems; connoisseurs of medieval legend and literature can follow in the footsteps of the Nibelungs; people interested in folklore can rediscover old legends and customs—and the rest of us can just relax and enjoy the magical setting and make explorations into the realms of the hearty Lower Austrian cooking.

The Wachau is easily accessible from Vienna by car—90 km (56 miles) on the motorway, or by Danube steamship. The best times to see this fascinating region are spring and autumn when the weather is mild and it is not too crowded.

A BRIEF HISTORY	
Prehistory	Archeological finds, such as the "Galgenberg Dancing Venus" and the "Willendorf Venus", prove that the Wachau was already inhabited in the Paleolithic.
1st century BC	The Danube forms the northern border of the Roman Empire. The Romans make improvements to viniculture, introduced to the Wachau by the Celts.
4th century AD	Goths, Huns and Avars from the Asian steppes invade the Danube basin.
7th century	Christianity reaches the Wachau via Salzburg.

A BRIEF HISTORY

9th century	In 823 the name "Wahowa" is first used for a small part of the Wachau.
10th century	Shipping flourishes on the Danube: wine, salt and wood are transported up- and downriver. The Babenbergs make Melk their royal residence.
11th–13th centuries	The Crusades herald a boom for the towns on the banks of the Danube. The robber barons also get their share. In 1192, England's Richard the Lion-Heart, on his way back from the Third Crusade, is imprisoned in the Kuenringerburg above Dürnstein. He is discovered by his minstrel and released after payment of a ransom. Part of the 13th-century *Song of the Nibelungs* is set in the Wachau. Melk is mentioned as "Medelike".
14th century	In 1338, a plague of locusts destroys the entire fruit harvest of the Wachau.
15th century	During the war against Hungary, Krems is besieged by King Matthias Corvinus, and the other towns of the Wachau also suffer.
16th century	War against the Turks. A major fire sweeps Krems in 1529, and in 1548 the town of Melk is almost totally destroyed by a blaze. It is rebuilt in the Renaissance style.
17th century	During the Thirty Years' War, Swedish troops burn Dürnstein, leave the Kuenringerburg in ruins, and besiege Krems and Stein. In 1680 the Wachau is hit by a catastrophic plague.
18th century	Jakob Prandtauer is commissioned to rebuild the abbey of Melk. After his death, his pupil Josef Munggenast completes the work. The parish church of Krems is also built at this time.
19th century	In 1829 the Danube Steamship Company *(Donau-Dampfschifffahrtsgesellschaft)* is founded. Until World War I it is the biggest inland shipping company in the world.
20th century	In 1929 the Danube freezes as far as Spitz in the Wachau. In 1972 a bridge is built over the Danube near Melk (previously the river could only be crossed here by ferry).

Sightseeing

Melk

Mentioned in the *Song of the Nibelungs* as "Medelike", Melk was settled as early as the 9th century, but was not to receive a charter until 1898. In the Middle Ages, the salt, wine and iron trades flourished here. In 1548 a fire reduced the town virtually to ashes, and the buildings were rebuilt in the Renaissance style. (The baroque façades date from the 18th century.)

After a short walk around the town, follow the Stiftsweg leading up to the magnificent Benedictine abbey, Stift Melk. Having crossed the forecourt, you find yourself confronted by the impressive eastern façade of the monastery. Via the Prälatenhof (Prelates' Court) you reach a magnificent staircase which climbs to the **Kaiserzimmer** (Imperial Rooms). In the museum here you can acquaint yourself with the secular and spiritual history of the abbey.

The **Marmorsaal** (Marble Hall), light, bright and richly decorated with ceiling frescoes and other ornaments, was used as a dining room and guest room in former days. Pass through the balconies to the **Bibliothek**, its magnificent inlaid shelves weighed down with some 80,000 precious books and 2000 manuscripts. Richly decorated with frescoes, the room is a work of art in its own right.

A spiral staircase leads down into the **Stiftskirche** (Abbey Church), where you can admire the high altar, the pulpit, the beautifully carved confessionals and choir stalls, the ceiling frescoes by Johann Michael Rottmayr and the great organ.

Amongst the showpieces of the **Schatzkammer** (Treasury) is the famous Cross of Melk inlaid with pearls and precious stones, and celebrated in legend. It is claimed that the cross was stolen in the 12th century. It found its way back to the monastery by mysterious means —floating against the current upstream from Vienna!

Dürnstein

This pretty little baroque town nestles on the bank of the Danube and can only be explored on foot: you have to leave your car on the edge of town.

Dürnstein is famous mainly for the **Kuenringerburg**, the castle in which Richard I of England, the Lion-Heart, was held captive in the 12th century. He had offended the Babenberg Duke Leopold V during the Third Crusade, and was recognized and captured in Vienna whilst attempting to slip away

Exqisite painting adorns the ceiling of Melk abbey's library.

up the Danube valley. According to the legend, his faithful minstrel Blondel traced him here to Dürnstein by singing the king's favourite songs outside every castle until he came to the right one and heard Richard join in the chorus. After the Swedish onslaught in 1645, only ruins remained of the castle. The ascent takes about 20 minutes and is rewarded with breathtaking views of the Danube.

The **Stiftskirche** (Monastic Church), resplendent in blue and white, has one of the finest baroque towers in the whole of Austria. Walk through the ornate portal and the quiet courtyard to reach the interior, where the three divine virtues Faith, Hope and Charity watch over the carved pulpit (and over the portal). The cloister is worth a visit.

On Hauptstrasse, bounded to the east by the Kremser Tor, you can see many pretty **town houses** from the 16th to 18th centuries, some of them with sgraffito decoration. On the same street, you will find the late-Gothic **Rathaus** (town hall) with its fine courtyard. Only ruins remain of the former **Klarissinenkloster** (Convent of the Poor Clares).

You can take part in a wine tasting in the **Kellerschlössl** (1715), with its huge old wine cellar and rich decoration of frescoes and reliefs.

For time out from sightseeing, try wandering along the picturesque banks of the Danube, or enjoy a good cup of coffee or a glass of wine on the terrace of a riverside café.

Krems

The centre of the Wachau's wine industry is considered to be the most beautiful town in Lower Austria. Krems and the neighbouring town of Stein, linked by the appropriately named village of Und ("and" in German), have merged together as they have grown in size.

If you walk westwards along Untere Landstrasse, past the Kleines Sgraffitohaus, you will come to the **Simandlbrunnen** "Simon's Fountain), depicting the character in question returning home from an evening's drinking to a none-too-gentle reception from his angry wife.

Cross Wegscheid to reach **Hoher Markt**, the town's oldest square. Here stands the resplendent Gothic **Gozzo-Burg**, built in the 13th century in Italian style by the municipal judge Gozzo. In the **Piaristenkirche**, the church in Piaristengasse, there's a particularly extensive collection of paintings by Martin Johann Schmidt (1718–1801), a prolific artist familiarly known as Kremser Schmidt, who adorned most of the region's churches. The **Pfarrkirche St. Veit** (St Vitus parish church) is a fine baroque building decorated by eminent artists. The large ceiling frescoes and the All Souls Altar, at the back of the church and to the right, are by Kremser Schmidt.

AUSTRIAN WINES

The Viennese are happy to drink white wine with either meat or fish. The best known of Austrian whites, Gumpoldskirchner, has the full body and bouquet of its southern vineyards. But the Viennese give equal favour to their own Grinzinger, Nussdorfer, Sieveringer and Neustifter. From the Danube valley, with an extra natural sparkle, come the Kremser, Dürnsteiner and Langenloiser.

To enjoy them to the full, visit a "Heuriger", a typically Austrian institution, where you drink young white wine and help yourself to a buffet of hot and cold snacks, usually including tasty cheese and cold meats, salads and crispy bread.

The former Dominican church today houses **museums** of history and viniculture. You will see sculptures from the medieval and baroque periods, paintings and etchings by Kremser Schmidt, and artefacts from the wine-growers' guild.

The **Stein Gate** at the end of Obere Landstrasse, was part of the medieval city wall. Its round Gothic towers date from the 15th century.

Steiner Landstrasse in **Stein** boasts several fine buildings. The **Minoritenkirche** (Minorites' Church) was built during the transition from Romanesque to Gothic, and this stylistic blend gives the building its particular character. The **Pfarrhof** (presbytery), with its magnificent rococo stucco work, is also worth a visit. The mighty seven-storey tower of the Frauenbergkirche rises above the town.

Dining Out

In the Wachau you may as well cast any good intentions to the winds and indulge yourself to the full on local specialities.

Among typical main courses you will find hearty goulash (*Herrengulasch*), roast meats (*Rostbraten*) with garlic, and *Bauernschmaus*, which literally means "farmer's feast": bread dumplings, sauerkraut, meat and sausage. With the Danube on the doorstep, fish is an essential item on any menu: trout, zander (pike-perch), pike and carp are prepared in various mouthwatering ways. Side dishes invariably include dumplings, a Wachau speciality, along with the more usual rice and chips.

Lovers of hot puddings will find plenty to satisfy their appetites: *Kaiserschmarren* (a sort of pancake with raisins), and if you can face another dumpling, *Topfen-, Marillen-* and *Germknödel* (filled with apricots, curd cheese or plums), and much more besides.

To go with your "Jause" (afternoon cup of coffee) there are plenty of mouthwatering pastries and strudel, stuffed with poppy seeds, nuts, curd cheese or apricots.

Shopping

Craft products include pottery, embroidery work and jewellery. Small watercolours or copper-plate engravings of the local landscape make a charming gift for your friends or a memento if you want to spoil yourself. Dolls in traditional Wachau costume (*Dirndl*) with golden bonnets are a popular buy, and a good bottle of local wine or apricot schnapps, Marillenbrand, will go down well.

PRACTICAL INFORMATION

Banks and currency exchange. Open Monday–Friday 8 or 9 a.m.–3 or 3.30 p.m., until 5.30 p.m. on Thursdays. Small branches generally close for lunch, between 12.30 and 1.30 p.m. Money can also be changed at railway stations and post offices, and you'll have no problems finding a cash machine.

Climate. The Wachau's favoured climate means plenty of sunshine and mild temperatures. Spring starts here at the beginning of March! On the other hand, Vienna has a continental climate. Winters are often harsh, with occasional snow. In January and February the temperature may drop to –15 °C (–9°F). In summer it may climb to 30 °C (86 °F).

Clothing. People tend to dress elegantly for the theatre, concerts and the opera.

Credit cards. The major cards are accepted in hotels, restaurants and large shops.

Currency. The Euro, divided into 100 cents. Coins: 1, 2, 5, 10, 20 and 50 cents, 1 and 2 euros; banknotes: 5, 10, 20, 50, 100, 200 and 500 euros.

Ferries. Mostly in operation 7 a.m.–7 p.m. during the summer months. Car ferries operate at Spitz and Weissenkirchen.

Media. The principal foreign newspapers are sold in kiosks on the day of publication. Hotels usually have cable TV and the main English-language information channels such as BBC World and CNN.

Post offices. Open Monday–Friday 8 a.m.–noon and 2–6 p.m, Saturday 8–10 a.m. Not all post offices are open on Saturdays.

Safety. Do not carry large amounts of cash, and when you go sightseeing, leave your valuables and important documents in your hotel or cruise ship safe.

Shops. Most small shops are open Monday to Friday 9 a.m.–6 p.m. with a break for lunch. Food shops open at 8 a.m. Major department stores open 8 a.m.–6 p.m., but supermarkets close for about two hours at lunch time. Shops are closed on Saturday afternoons, except for the first Saturday of each month, when they remain open until 5 p.m., as well as Sundays.

Time. GMT + 1 in winter, GMT +2 from end March to end October.

Tipping. A service charge is automatically added to restaurant bills, but it is customary to round the bill up by about 10%. You should also leave a small tip in cafés.

VIENNA

City of Legends

As the old capital of the Habsburg empire—which included not only Slavs and Hungarians but also Germans, Spaniards, Italians and Belgians—Vienna has always been an outpost and gateway of Western civilization. A melting pot long before New York, the city has perpetually defied a simple national label. Its language is German—with a distinctive Viennese touch. But the city and people have too much Balkan and Latin in them to be compared with Hamburg, Berlin or Frankfurt.

The town's tree-lined Ringstrasse, encircling the Inner City, compares favourably with the airy sweep of Parisian boulevards. In every sense the heart of the city, it has baroque palaces, elegant shops, convivial cafés, the illustrious Burgtheater and Staatsoper (State Opera) and narrow medieval streets, winding around the cathedral.

Outside the Ring, the city sprawls through 22 other districts with plentiful parks and even farms and vineyards inside the city limits. Vienna has space to relax, a city in a rural setting that makes the attitude to life of its 1.5 million population more easygoing than in most modern cities.

This pleasant atmosphere always comes as a surprise to visitors. Most of the people still seem to have time for the courtesies of the old days. Shopkeepers like to call their regular customers by aristocratic titles that, constitutionally, should have disappeared after World War I, or at least by a nicely inflated professional title.

No word better describes the ideal of Viennese life than *Gemütlichkeit*. Literally untranslatable, *gemütlich* means agreeable, comfortable. As unmistakable as a Viennese smile, it is the quality that takes the rough edges off life.

A BRIEF HISTORY	
1st–3rd centuries	Romans set up a garrison—Vindobona—on the Danube and drive off successive invasions by Teutons, Slavs and other tribes. Emperor Marcus Aurelius leads fighting against the barbarians and dies in Vindobona in 180.
4th–12th centuries	Christianity is introduced; barbarian invasions continue. The Babenberg dynasty drives out the Magyars around 1000, and they are named hereditary Dukes of Austria by the Holy Roman Emperor in 1156.

13th century	Vienna's first "golden age" begins. Art, trade, and handicrafts thrive; Scottish and Irish monks establish a monastery; churches, residences and new thoroughfares are built. The last of the Babenbergs dies in 1246; Ottokar II of Bohemia succeeds to the regency. He is supplanted by Rudolf von Habsburg in 1278.
14th–16th centuries	Rudolf der Stifter (the Founder) creates the university in 1365. In 1469 Vienna is granted Rome's approval as a bishopric. Hungarian King Matthias Corvinus occupies the city from 1485 to 1490. In 1529 Turks under Suleiman the Magnificent lay siege. The Innere Stadt holds firm and Suleiman retreats. The Reformation reaches Vienna but Catholicism remains predominant.
17th century	Emperor Leopold I ushers Vienna into its glorious baroque era. The construction of magnificent palaces and churches begins. The plague strikes in 1679; the Turks lay a second unsuccessful siege in 1683.
18th century	Emperor Charles VI is succeeded by his daughter Maria Theresa. Her relatively benevolent 40-year reign extends its influence to the capital's citizens and Vienna blooms as a musical city.
19th century	Napoleon's armies arrive in 1805. Emperor Franz I gives his daughter Marie-Louise in diplomatic marriage to Napoleon in 1810. The Congress of Vienna completes its territorial discussions in June 1815 and provides Europe with a framework for international diplomacy which is to last a hundred years. The Ringstrasse complex of aristocratic residences is developed and the new opera built.
20th century	The Habsburg empire ends with World War I, which leaves Vienna in economic and social ruin. Chancellor Dollfuss is murdered by Austrian Nazis in 1934. Hitler annexes Austria and it becomes a province of "Greater Germany" from 1938 to 1945. After the war Vienna is divided into four sectors under the joint four-power administration of the Americans, Russians, British and French. In 1955 Austria is given independent neutral status and enters a prosperous new period of economic recovery. It joined the EU in 1994.

Sightseeing

The best way to appreciate the city centre is on foot, but for a more romantic introduction to the town, try a **Fiaker tour**. The two-horse open carriages have been in business since the 17th century, and their elegantly turned out drivers have a fund of amusing stories to put you in the right mood.

The cathedral, **Stephansdom**, will draw you like a magnet; it is the ideal starting point for your visit. With its Romanesque western façade, Gothic tower and baroque altars, the cathedral is a marvellous example of the Viennese genius for harmonious compromise, melding the austerity, dignity and exuberance of those great architectural styles. The Romanesque origins are visible in the Heidentürme and statuary depicting, among others, a griffin and Samson fighting a lion. The transformation into the Gothic structure we see today was carried out mainly during the 14th and 15th centuries.

From the north tower you have a fine view of the city, and of the huge Pummerin bell cast from melted-down Turkish cannons after the 1683 siege was repelled. The present bell is a recast version of the original destroyed during World War II.

Inside the church, look in the centre aisle for the charming carved Gothic **pulpit** by Anton Pilgram. At the head of the spiral staircase, the sculptor has placed Augustine, Gregory, Jerome and Ambrose, fathers of the Church. He also defied the customary medieval anonymity with a sculpture of himself looking through a window under the staircase.

On the left side of the high altar you'll find the carved wooden **Wiener Neustädter Altar**; on the right side is the impressive marble **tomb** of Emperor Friedrich III, honoured by the Viennese as the man who had the city made a bishopric.

After a long visit to the Stephansdom (and a coffee in one of the pleasant *Kaffeehaüser* in the area) head for the **Figarohaus** just southeast of the cathedral. Here, from 1784 to 1787, lived Wolfgang Amadeus Mozart; the house has been transformed into a museum devoted to the great composer. He wrote 11 of his piano concertos here, as well as the *Marriage of Figaro* and many other pieces. After struggling to finish the *Magic Flute* and the *Requiem*, he died a pauper in the musty Rauhensteingasse not far away. A department store now stands on the site of the house where he died. His coffin was blessed in an anonymous ceremony for that day's dead.

Stroll back to the **Kärntner Strasse**, the city's main north-south thoroughfare where many of Vienna's smartest shops can be found. Today it is a traffic-free pedestrian zone with open-air cafés down the middle of the street. At the Stephansdom end of Kärntner Strasse pass through the Stock-im-Eisen square to the **Graben**, also a pedestrian zone. The **Pestsäule** (Pillar of the Plague) is a somewhat grotesque monument commemorating the town's deliverance from the plague in 1679.

The **Peterskirche** (St Peter's Church), just off the Graben, provides a splendid example of how Viennese baroque manages more often than not to be both sumptuous and intimate. Designed by Johann Lukas, it has an unusual oval-shaped nave. The curved pews are all decorated with three sculpted angels.

From here you can make a short detour through the old Jewish quarter to the **Ruprechts-kirche**, easily recognizable by its ivy-covered façade.

Return to the **Hoher Markt**, which was the forum of the Roman settlement, Vindobona. A small museum displays the remains of two Roman houses laid bare by a 1945 bombardment.

To the west, follow Salvator-gasse, pausing to admire the superb Renaissance porch of the **Salvatorkapelle**, a happy marriage of Italian design and Austrian late-Gothic sculpture. Beyond it is a slender jewel of 14th-century Gothic, the church of **Maria am Gestade** ("Mary on the Banks"—of the River Danube that used to flow directly beneath it).

Walk back across the Juden-platz to the spacious **Am Hof**, the largest square of the old city. An elaborate baroque building makes a grand fire station. From here make for the **Freyung** triangle flanked by the **Schot-tenkirche** (Scots' Church), founded by Scottish and Irish Benedictine monks in the 12th century.

Ring

Before tackling the Hofburg, it's a good idea to go around the Ring, probably the greatest single urban achievement of Franz Joseph. This boulevard encircling the Innere Stadt was mapped out in the 1860s along the ramparts Joseph II had begun clearing 80 years before.

Start your walk at the west end of the Schottenring, in front of the **Votivkirche**, a neo-Gothic church built after Franz Joseph survived an assassination attempt in 1853. Next to it 35

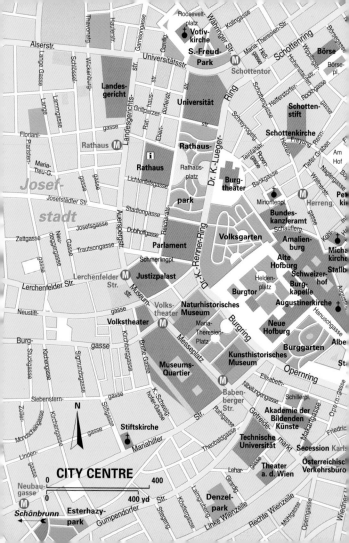

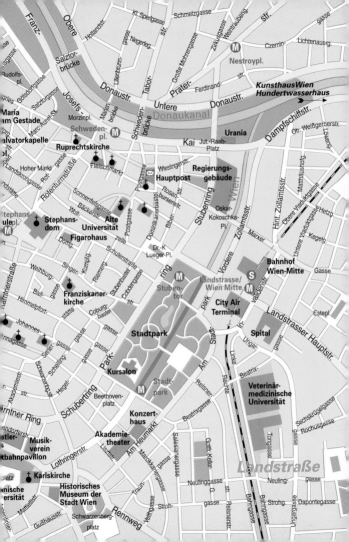

are the university and **Rathaus** (Town Hall) with a pleasant park, but proceed along the Innere Stadt side, past the impressive **Burgtheater**, a high temple of the German stage. Beyond it is the lovely **Volksgarten**. Its cafés and open-air concerts carry on a tradition that began with the café music of the Strauss family.

The **Burggarten**, the park of Hofburg, leads to the **Staatsoper** (State Opera). It's worth taking a guided tour here before attending a performance.

On Karlsplatz, not far from the opera house, stands the huge **Karlskirche**, undoubtedly the most important of the city's baroque churches. Its visual impact has diminished since the building of the Ringstrasse. However, the cool, sober interior remains unchanged, with a subdued marble decor and an oval ground-plan similar to that of the Peterskirche. In front of the

church, a massive Henry Moore sculpture in a reflector pool provides a striking contrast. Also on the Karlsplatz is Otto Wagner's fanciful **Stadtbahnpavillon** (an old underground station) with its graceful green, gold and white Jugendstil motif of sunflowers and tulips. Close by you will notice a house with a golden cupola, built in 1898 by architect Joseph Maria Olbrich. In the basement is a frieze by Gustav Klimt, inspired by Beethoven.

The Hofburg

Though the Habsburgs are long gone, Vienna remains an imperial city—an aura enhanced by its palaces.

The most imposing is the Hofburg, home of Austria's rulers since the 13th century. Start your visit right in the middle at the **Schweizerhof**, named after the Swiss Guard that used to be housed there. Here Ottokar of Bohemia built a fortress in 1275–76 to defend himself against Rudolf von Habsburg. He wasn't successful and the Habsburgs moved in; they strengthened the fortifications because of the unruly Viennese outside.

The **Burgkapelle** (Castle Chapel), tucked away in the northern corner of the Schweizerhof, was built in 1449. Originally Gothic, it was redone in baroque style and then partially restored to its original form in 1802. The Vienna Boys' Choir (Wiener Sängerknaben) sings Mass here every Sunday morning, except in July and August.

Between 1558 and 1565 Ferdinand I built the **Stallburg** (outside the main Hofburg complex on the northeast side of Reitschulgasse) as a home for his son Archduke Maximilian.

Still in Renaissance style is Rudolf II's **Amalienburg**, built

HISTORY OF SCHÖNBRUNN

Like many monarchs of his time, Leopold I wanted his new palace to surpass the magnificence and grandeur of Louis XIV's Versailles. In 1683, the Turkish siege had left Schloss Schönbrunn in ruins and Johann Bernhard Fischer von Erlach was commissioned to build the new summer residence. Nonetheless, a first project was rejected as too ambitious and too costly. A "more modest" choice was made with only 1,441 rooms. Construction continued till 1730.

Maria Theresa had the palace expanded in 1750 according to the plan of Nicolaus Pacassi. Thus the interior rooms received a new décor, new gardens were landscaped and the Empress opened in 1752 Europe's first zoological garden. On the hill overlooking the palace the Gloriette pavilion was built as a triumphal arch to commemorate the Austrian victory over the Prussians in 1757.

Schönbrunn's architecture marks the ascendancy of the more playfully ornate rococo over baroque. The glowing "Schönbrunn Yellow" of the buildings was copied throughout the empire on villas and palaces. Marie-Antoinette spent her youth here. Napoleon made it his headquarters in 1805 and again in 1809. His son, the Duke of Reichstadt, died here in 1832. Franz Joseph was born in Schönbrunn in 1830 and it was here that he died in 1916. In the palace's Blue Chinese Room, the last Habsburg emperor, Karl I, signed his abidcation decree on November 11, 1918.

between 1575 and 1611, mostly by Italian architect Pietro Ferrabosco.

Leopold I launched the city's baroque era with his **Leopoldinischer Trakt** (Leopold Wing), which now serves as the home of the Austrian presidency.

Karl VI continued the Habsburg's self-confident traditions with the **Reichskanzlei** (Imperial Chancellery), where Franz Joseph was later to have his apartments, the Hofbibliothek (library) and the Winterreitschule (the winter quarters of the Spanish Riding School).

Josefsplatz is a marvellously harmonious baroque square, with an equestrian statue of Joseph II in the middle. Inside the old library, the oval **Prunksaal** (Great Hall), with frescoes and walnut bookshelves, is one

---

SISSI: MYTH AND REALITY

In the 1950s, the cinema drew a picture of Sissi that was kitschy and divorced from all reality. Empress Elisabeth (1837–98) was an intelligent and cultivated woman who worried little about court etiquette and much about the destiny of the Hungarian people. She spent a long time in the vicinity of Budapest. The sensitive empress was very much concerned about her physical appearance. For this she imposed iron discipline with exercise and a constant diet. From her 30th birthday, she refused to let herself be photographed.

After her marriage with her cousin Franz Joseph at the age of 16, she had to exchange a hitherto fairly free life in Bavaria for the strict supervision of her mother-in-law, Sophie, who also later took over the education of the children. The empress fell ill and took refuge in the milder climate of Madeira—the first of a long series of journeys abroad.

In June 1867, her efforts for more recognition for the Hungarian people reaped their reward. The imperial couple were crowned King and Queen of Hungary: the dual monarchy was born. Even this, however, did not keep Sissi in the palace. After she had given her husband four children, she decided at 40 to distance herself still further from court and pursue her passion for poetry and travel.

The empress suffered a terrible blow when her son, Rudolf committed suicide. In 1889, in mysterious circumstances, the heir to the throne took his life, along with that of his mistress, Baroness Mary Vetsera, on the royal estate of Mayerling. Nine years later, when out walking on the Quai du Mont-Blanc in Geneva, Elisabeth was stabbed to death by the Italian anarchist Luigi Lucheni.

Mermaid's view of the elegant Schloss Schönbrunn.

of the most beautiful baroque interiors in the world.

Just off the Josefsplatz is the **Augustinerkirche**, the church that the Habsburgs favoured for their great events. The façade of this Gothic and baroque structure matches the library and Redoutensaal. The church they chose to be buried in, the Kapuzinerkirche, lies outside the Hofburg. Its **Kaisergruft** (Imperial Vault) contains some 140 assorted Habsburgs—emperors, empresses, archdukes and less exalted members of the family.

The **Spanische Reitschule** (Spanish Riding School) must not be missed, even if it is just to see the splendid arcades sup-

ported by 46 columns. The white Lippizaner horses are trained to walk and dance with a delicacy that many ballet-dancers might envy. Tickets for performances must be booked at least six months in advance; a more convenient option is to watch the horses train.

For an idea of the human scale of what turned into the Habsburgs' folly, you should take the 45-minute guided tour of the **Imperial Apartments** *(Kaiserappartements)*, entrance on Michaelerplatz.

When you leave the Hofburg, take the Schauflergasse to **Ballhausplatz** to see the elegant 18th-century residence of the 41

Austrian chancellors. One of them, Dollfuss, was assassinated here in July 1934.

Schönbrunn

If the Hofburg is the oversized expression of a dynasty that outgrew its own virility, Schönbrunn is the smiling, serene expression of the personality of one woman—Maria Theresa, Archduchess of Austria, Queen of Bohemia and Hungary.

SACHERTORTE

Franz Sacher created this rich chocolate cake for a gala dinner in honour of Chancellor Metternich in 1832. Traditionally it is covered with a thick glossy layer of dark chocolate icing and has a filling of a thin layer of apricot jam. It is often served with whipped cream. It can be ordered from Hotel Sacher, Philharmonikerstrasse 4, or by telephone, (1) 514 560; they send it all over the world securely packed in smart wooden boxes. Other cafés—for example, at the Hotel Imperial and Demel—make their own claims to superiority. A story is told of an absentminded American who left his papers in the famous hotel, forgetting both its name and its address. He sent a telegram to "Hotel Chocolate Cake, Vienna". It was duly delivered to Sacher.

To appreciate the emphasis that Schönbrunn puts on pleasure, rather than imperial pomp, it's best to visit the **gardens** first. The park, laid out in the classical French manner, is dominated by the **Gloriette**, a neoclassical colonnade perched on the crest of a hill. It commemorates the Austrian victory of 1757 over Frederick II's Prussian army. Today it houses a café.

East of the Neptune Fountain are the bizarre **Roman ruins**, actually built in 1778—a half-buried "Roman palace" with bits of Corinthian columns, friezes and archways.

After visiting the gardens head for the **palace**, where a guided grand tour (audioguides also available) will give you a glimpse of the sumptuous comfort in which Maria Theresa and her successors handled the affairs of state. For those in a hurry, a short tour takes in only the appartments of Franz-Josef and his wife Sissi in the right wing. On the long tour you'll see Maria Theresa's breakfast room, decorated with the needlework of the empress and her myriad daughters; the **Spiegelsaal** (Hall of Mirrors) in which the young Mozart gave his first royal recital; the **Chinesisches Rundkabinett** (Chinese Round Room), superbly adorned with lacquered Oriental panels, and also known as Maria Theresa's Konspirationstafelstube (roughly translatable as "dining room for plotting").

You should not miss what is known as the **Napoleon Room** (though it was once Maria Theresa's bedroom), where the emperor stayed on his way to the Battle of Austerlitz and where his son, the Duke of Reichstadt, spent his last sad years.

In the adjoining **Wagenburg** museum, you can marvel at a collection of coaches used by the imperial court.

Belvedere

Of all the palaces built by the princes, dukes and barons serving the Habsburgs, the most splendid must certainly be the Belvedere of Prince Eugene of Savoy. It is regarded as Vienna's finest flowering of baroque residential architecture.

Today the **Unteres Belvedere** and its **Orangerie** house the admirable collections of Austrian medieval and baroque art in the Barockmuseum. On the other side of the park, in the **Oberes** (or Upper) **Belvedere**, the prince held his banquets and

A QUICK COFFEE?

Not likely. In Vienna a coffee is to be savoured slowly, not swallowed down in one gulp. The choice is confusingly large. Here are a few explanations:

Brauner: black with a dash of milk.

Einspänner: black with whipped cream, served in a tall glass.

Eiskaffee: black with whipped cream and vanilla ice cream.

Kapuziner: cappuccino, topped

with a dollop of whipped cream and sprinkled with powdered chocolate.

Melange: frothy and milky, maybe with a blob of whipped cream.

Mocca: strong and black, most often espresso.

Türkischer: boiling hot and sweet.

other festivities. Nowhere will you see a finer view of the city skyline than from its **terrace**, which has changed little since Bellotto-Canaletto painted it in 1760.

The Other Vienna

Beyond the Innere Stadt and outside the Habsburg world of the Hofburg and Schönbrunn, there is another Vienna, the people's Vienna.

Cross the Danube Canal over the Aspernbrücke, at the junction of Franz-Josefs-Kai and Stubenring. This takes you to the **Prater** park, Vienna's own non-stop carnival (also accessible by tram or underground). If the Stephansdom had not already become the undisputed symbol of the city, the Prater's **Riesenrad** (giant Ferris wheel) built in 1897 would certainly have laid a claim. Immortalized by Carol Reed's film *The Third Man* (1949), the Riesenrad, with its 14 bright red cabins taking you up for a constantly changing perspective of the city's skyline, is only part of the fair that includes roller-coasters, discotheques, shooting ranges, restaurants and beer halls.

The **Donaupark** linking the old and new Danube is more tranquil than the Prater, laid out with beautiful flower beds, and artificial lake, sports arenas and

CAPITAL OF MUSIC

Austrian music, subject to Mediterranean as well as Germanic influences, has always had a seductive elegance. The musical renown of Vienna lasted from the last third of the 18th century to the first half of the 20th, from Haydn to Webern. During this time an impressive number of musicians were active in Vienna: Gluck, Haydn, Mozart, Beethoven, Schubert, Strauss, Bruckner, Brahms, Mahler, Wolf, Schönberg, Berg and many others.

Vienna evolved in the second half of the 18th century, with Haydn and Mozart, to Europe's music capital. Like the Esterhazy family, who commissioned symphonies and masses from Haydn, princes competed for the privilege of financing a composer who would in exchange dedicate to them some of their works. Johann Strauss transformed a plodding German dance into the gay, whirling waltz which soon took the city by storm. His son, also Johann, became known as the Waltz King.

At the beginning of the 20th century, Gustav Mahler breathed new life into the town as conductor of the Philharmonic. With its 12-tone music, the Second Vienna School brought about a musical revolution.

a chair-lift from which to survey it all. It also features a 250-m (827-ft) tower, the **Donauturm**, with two revolving restaurants and a public terrace featuring a view across the city south to the hills of the Wienerwald and northwest to the Abbey of Klosterneuburg.

Döbling is the most gracious of Vienna's neighbourhoods. Stretching from the Danube Canal back to the undulating slopes of the Wienerwald, Döbling includes Sievering, Grinzing, Heiligenstadt, Nussdorf and Kahlenberg. It has elegant villas, parks, vineyards and, of course, the ever popular Heurigen wine gardens.

A short detour to the north takes in the imposing Augustine abbey of **Klosterneuburg**, founded in the 12th century. The baroque palace-church is impressive but the trip is made worthwhile by the magnificent **Verdun Altar** of 1181, containing 45 enamelled panels depicting scenes from the scriptures.

Museums

Vienna's National Gallery, the **Kunsthistorisches Museum**, is outstanding. The magnificent collection contains masterpieces by all of the European great masters—Dutch, Flemish, German and English to the left and Italian, Spanish and French to

the right. Its twin, the **Naturhistorische Museum**, has zoological, anthropological, paleontological displays and a beautiful collection of gemstones.

Nearby, the modern **MuseumsQuartier** was inaugurated in 2001. It is one of the 10 biggest cultural complexes in the world, with several museums, theatres and exhibition halls.

Austrian art is displayed in three different galleries of the **Belvedere**: the museum of medieval art, the baroque museum, and the gallery of 19th and 20th century art, with works by Klimt, Schiele, Kokoschka, Munch and others.

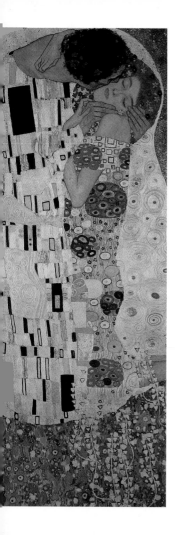

You can also admire 20th-century works in the **Museum des 20. Jahrhunderts** in the Schweizergaren, near the Belvedere.

Most of the vast Habsburg fortune can be seen in the Hofburg. The **Schatzkammer** (Treasury), in the Schweizerhof, contains a dazzling display of the insignia of the old Holy Roman Empire. These include the Imperial Crown of pure unalloyed gold, set with pearls and unpolished emeralds, sapphires and rubies. The **Hoftafel und Silberkammer** (Court

GUSTAV KLIMT

Klimt (1862–1918) was one of the pioneers of modern painting in Vienna. In 1897 he became the first president of the Secession group, which gathered a number of young artists in search of new means of expression. Having assimilated the innovative ideas and spirit of the Impressionists, Symbolists and Pre-Raphaelites, as well as the precepts of Art Nouveau, he developed a powerful personal style, at once opulent and disquieting. Among his major works, *The Kiss* is displayed at the Belvedere, while his 34-m long Beethoven frieze can be seen in the basement of the Secession pavilion.

China and Silver Collection) exhibits the priceless Chinese, Japanese, French Sèvres and German Meissen services amassed by the Habsburgs over six centuries.

You can visit the Schubert, Haydn, Beethoven or Mozart museums, but the best arranged of these "personal" museums, making up for the hostility with which most Viennese received him during his lifetime, is the one devoted to **Sigmund Freud**. The house that he lived in at Berggasse 19 before he had to flee the Nazis has become a mecca for students—and patients—of psychoanalysis from all over the world.

The Vienna-born painter and architect Friedensreich Hundertwasser created the bizarre design for the **KunstHaus-Wien**, on Untere Weissgerberstr. 13 in the 3rd district, using recycled material and pieces of brightly coloured ceramics. In contrast to the severity and austerity of Vienna's architecture, there are no straight lines anywhere, and everything seems slightly skewed. Despite its confusing style—or because of it—this small, private gallery is worth a visit.

The **Hundertwasser-Haus**, an apartment block on Löwengasse in the 3rd district, is another shining example of non-conformism and environmental awareness. For the façade, recycled bricks and other materials were used. No two windows are alike. A 5-km (3-mile) ceramic strip circles the façade and two onion-shaped cupolas adorn the roof. Hundertwasser also designed schools and churches, a spa, a motorway restaurant and a municipal rubbish dump incinerator, in a similar unorthodox style.

Dining Out

The emperors, archdukes and generals have gone; not so the Bohemian dumplings, Hungarian goulash, Polish stuffed cabbage and Serbian shashlik. But there are Austrian specialities too: *Wienerschnitzel*, a large thinly sliced cutlet of veal crisply sauteed in a coating of egg and seasoned breadcrumbs; *Backhendl*, boned deep-fried chicken prepared like *Wienerschnitzel; Tafelspitz*, boiled beef, a Viennese favourite; or *Knödel*, dumplings served with soups and with the meat dish, studded with pieces of liver or bacon.

Dumplings are also served as a dessert with hot apricot inside (*Marillenknödel*) or with cream cheese (*Topfenknödel*). Another delicious pudding is *Apfelstrudel*, thinly sliced apple with raisins and cinnamon rolled in an almost transparent, flaky pastry. As for pastries: the word is almost inseparable from Vienna itself, like "waltz", "woods", and "Danube". The variations of cherries, strawberries, hazelnuts, walnuts, apple and chocolate in tarts, pies and cakes are endless. Have them topped with whipped cream (*mit Schlag*) or without, but do have them—your coffee would not be the same without. And join in the never-ending controversy over the most famous chocolate cake in the world, the *Sachertorte*—whether it should be split and sandwiched together with apricot jam, or just left plain.

Shopping

Not surprisingly, the most important shopping attraction in Vienna—a town preoccupied by its history—is antiques. Furniture and objets d'art from all over the old empire have somehow ended up here in the little shops in the Innere Stadt.

Still in the realm of the past are the great speciality shops for coin and stamp-collectors (where else could you expect to find mint-condition Bosnia-Herzegovina issues of 1914?).

The national Augarten porcelain workshops still turn out hand-decorated rococo chinaware. Exquisite petitpoint embroidery is available in the form of handbags, cushions and other items with flower, folk and opera motifs. You will find the more elegant shops on the Kärntnerstrasse, Graben and Kohlmarkt.

If your taste runs from the exquisite to kitsch, try your luck in the Saturday morning flea market on the Naschmarkt, with plenty of food stalls, too.

BRATISLAVA

Proud Fortress

Unlike other European capitals, the mention of Bratislava may not send people into raptures. But upon closer examination, the city reveals plenty of cultural and historical interest.

The German Pressburg, Hungarian Pozsony and Slovakian Bratislava are in fact one and the same place, its successive names testifying to a rich and varied past. Many influences have contributed to the culture of the Slovak capital, the most important being the Magyar. Bratislava was the Hungarian capital for 250 years and many Austro-Hungarian monarchs were crowned here. The Czech influence is also felt, as until 1 January 1993, the Czech and Slovak republics formed one state, in which Bratislava was subordinate to Prague.

Bratislava's geographical location has always played a part in the vicissitudes of its history.

About 60 km (37 miles) from Vienna and 200 km (124 miles) from Budapest, the city lies on the banks of the Danube, where Slovakia meets Austria and Hungary, at the foot of the Little Carpathians.

To this day, Bratislava, with 450,000 inhabitants, is one of the Danube's major ports. It has developed into an important industrial centre and venue for trade fairs. The cultural and economic focus of Slovakia, Bratislava boasts such great institutions as the Slovak Academy of the Sciences, founded in 1465 by the Hungarian King Matthias Corvinus, a conservatory and a theatre academy.

With Renaissance, baroque and rococo buildings, the Old Quarter holds a great deal of charm for visitors; those with a passion for culture and the arts will find a wealth of theatres and museums. Jazz and classical music festivals attract music lovers from all over the world.

A BRIEF HISTORY

3rd century BC– 2nd century AD	The area occupied by modern Slovakia is settled by Celts, who are driven out by Germanic tribes in the 1st century BC. Towards the end of the 2nd century AD, these in their turn are ousted by the Romans under Marcus Aurelius. (The Hungarian name Pozsony is derived from the Roman Posonium.)
6th century	In the wake of Germanic tribes and Huns, Slavs settle in the Danube basin.

A BRIEF HISTORY

9th century	The Great Moravian Duke Bratislav (after whom Bratislava is named) builds a castle above the Danube.
10th–12th centuries	In 907 the town is mentioned as "Brezalauspure" (later Pressburg). After the demise of the Great Moravian Empire under the onslaught of the Magyars, Slovakia falls to Hungary. German immigrants influence the development of towns and mining.
13th century	In 1291 King Andrew III of Hungary grants Pressburg (German at that time) the rights of a free royal city.
15th century	In 1465 a Hungarian university is founded. In the Treaty of Pressburg (1491) with King Vladislav II of Bohemia, the Habsburg Holy Roman Emperor Maximilian I establishes his family's succession to the thrones of Hungary and Bohemia.
16th century	The city flourishes. After the Turks' invasion of Hungary, Bratislava becomes the capital of Habsburg Hungary in 1541 and remains so for some 250 years; the monarchs are crowned in St Martin's Cathedral.
18th century	The city enjoys a renaissance under the rule of Maria Theresa: magnificent baroque palaces are built. However, in 1783 Joseph II transfers the capital back to Buda, and Bratislava's importance declines.
19th century	After the Battle of Austerlitz, Napoleon and Franz I of Austria sign the Peace of Pressburg (1805). From 1825–48 the Hungarian parliament is held in the city. The Slovaks make their national and social demands heard, but Slovakia still remains subject to Hungary.
20th century	Czechoslovakia comes into being in 1918. From 1939–45 Slovakia is independent, but maintains close ties with the German Reich. In April 1945 Soviet troops capture Bratislava, and in May Slovakia is handed back to the Prague government. After the peaceful separation of the Czech and Slovak Republics, Bratislava becomes capital of Slovakia on the first of January 1993. Far-reaching privatization of state concerns takes place. Since its separation from the Czech Republic, Slovakia has been forging stronger economic links with the West. Slovakia will join the EU in 2004.

Sightseeing

Castle (Hrad)

Visible from afar, this majestic building with its four corner towers stands prominently on a hill above the Danube. The fortress was built in the Middle Ages, but alterations took place in the 17th and 18th centuries. It was destroyed by fire in 1811 and rebuilt only after 1953. Those rooms accessible to the public hold part of the collections of the Slovakian National Museum, the Treasury and an exhibition which illustrates the history of the castle and of Slovakia. (The remaining rooms are used as government offices.)

The **Castle Gardens**, created in the reign of Maria Theresa, offer a breathtaking view of the Old Quarter and the Danube.

Old Quarter

Leave the gardens by the Gothic Corvinus Gate, and descend the Castle Steps (Zámocké schody) to the Old Quarter. In its narrow streets, ideal for exploring on foot, you'll discover Gothic, Renaissance and baroque palaces, churches and historical monuments round almost every corner.

The Castle Steps open onto Beblavého Street, which boasts the finest rococo building in the city: the **House of the Good Shepherd** (Dom u dobrého pastiera). Here you'll find an interesting clock museum.

Diagonally opposite on the expressway (use the subway!), you'll see the 14th-century **St Martin's Cathedral** (Dóm sv. Martina). With its three naves, it is one of the most beautiful examples of Gothic architecture in the whole of Slovakia. Between the years 1563 and 1830, 19 Austro-Hungarian monarchs were crowned here, a fact commemorated by the golden crown which tops the cathedral spire. The generously proportioned interior has been altered many times in the course of the centuries. The impressive bronze of St Martin, the city's patron saint, is the work of the famous Viennese sculptor Donner.

From the cathedral, take the pretty route along Panská Street, lined with neat Renaissance and baroque palaces, to the Main Square. During the restoration of the **Pálffy Palace** (Pálfyho palác), archaeological remains from Great Moravian and even Celtic times were discovered. These finds are displayed here alongside works of art from the City Gallery.

The palaces around **Main Square** (Hlavné námestie) bear witness to its former greatness. Of particular interest is the **Old Town Hall** (Stará radnica) on

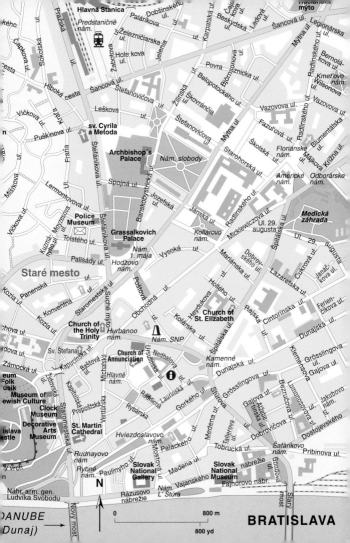

the eastern side of the square, the city's oldest secular building (1325). Public functions take place in the courtyard here during the yearly summer festival. The building also houses the extensive collections of the **City Museum** *(Mestské múzeum)*, which will better acquaint you with the history of Bratislava from its origins to the present day. Take a look also at the Renaissance Roland's Fountain (1572) in front of the Town Hall.

If you head in a northeasterly direction, you will come shortly to the **Primate's Palace** *(Primaciálny palác)* on the square of the same name. This powerful neoclassical building was constructed at the end of the 18th century. In its Mirror Hall, Napoleon and Emperor Franz I of Austria signed the Treaty of Pressburg after the Battle of Austerlitz. Part of the art collection of the City Gallery can be found here.

Just a few steps further on stands the house in which the composer Johann Nepomuk Hummel was born. Today it is a **museum** with documents and artefacts from his life.

Return now to Franciscan Square *(Františkánske námestie)*, which adjoins Main Square to the north. The principal points of interest here are the

baroque 17th-century **Jesuit Church** *(Kostol jezuitov)* and the Gothic **Franciscan Church** *(Kostol františkánov)*, the oldest building in the town centre. It has been altered many times, and was given a baroque façade in the 18th century. The Gothic Chapel of St John was left untouched.

Opposite stands the magnificent rococo **Mirbach Palace** *(Mirbachov palác)*. The inner courtyard with its 19th-century fountain makes an attractive venue for concerts. Within the palace there's a gallery of paintings, together with six marvellous 17th-century tapestries.

Heading in a westerly direction, you come to **St Michael's Gate** *(Michalská brána)*, part of the former fortifications of the city. The tower, now 51 m (167 ft) high, has grown since it was first built at the beginning of the 14th century, as extrastoreys were added over the years. In 1758 the tower was crowned with a baroque cupola, upon which St Michael sits enthroned. From the top, you have a fine view of the old town.

On the corner of Huranovo and Októbrové squares are the baroque **Church of the Holy Trinity** *(Kostol trinitárov)* and its monastery (1715–25).

A flight of steps leads to the picturesque old Klariská Street and the **Church of the Poor Clares** *(Kostol Klarisiek)*, with a late-Gothic belltower that provides a conspicuous landmark in the old town. This church, too, has been altered many times, and today it is the venue for concerts and functions.

Crossing narrow Bastová Street, you arrive at Michalská and then Ventúrska streets, which lead down to the Danube. In former times, these streets were mainly used as a thoroughfare by merchants, but now they are lined with shops, bars and restaurants—alongside historical buildings such as the baroque University Library, which until 1848 was the home of the Hungarian parliament. The building that once housed the **Academia Istropolitana**—the first Hungarian (or Slovak) university, founded in 1465—is now occupied by the Music Academy.

Major theatres, museums and hotels are grouped in the elegant district between the Danube *(Dunaj)* and the greenery of wide Hviezdoslavovo Square. At its eastern end stands the **Slovak National Theatre** *(Slovenské národné divadlo)*, built in 1886 in neo-Renaissance style.

Operas and concerts are performed nearby in the **Reduta Palace**, the home of the Slovak Philharmonic Orchestra.

Directly on the bank of the Danube, you'll find two interesting museums, the **Slovak National Gallery** *(Slovenská národná galéria)* with older and contemporary art, and the **Slovak National Museum** *(Slovenská národné múzeum)* displaying botanical, mineralogical and other exhibits.

The modern **Danube bridge** *(Most SNP*—Bridge of the Slovak National Uprising) has a single 86-m (282-ft) column, at the top of which is perched a panoramic restaurant, overlooking both old and new towns.

Dining Out

Slav and Hungarian influences intermingle in Slovak cuisine. Generally speaking, dishes are good and inexpensive, nourishing and often strongly spiced. As well as the restaurant *(restaurace)*, there's the wine cellar *(vináreň)* and—for lovers of coffee and the sweet things in life—the café and cake shop *(cukráreň)*.

Try the following specialities: spicy beef goulash *à la* Bratislava or fiery shish kebabs with pork, beef and lamb (together with ham, sausage, peppers and onions). Side dishes include potato concoctions like dumplings. Smoked cheese is another speciality, fried with ham and served with tartare sauce.

To drink, try beer *(pivo)* or wine *(víno)*. Local wines are mostly from the Veltliner, Sylvaner and Riesling grape varieties, and have sonorous names such as *Malokarpatské zlato* ("Gold from the Little Carpathians"). Then there are all sorts of spirits, like *borovicka* (gin-like), *slivovica* (plum brandy) or *marhulovica* (apricot brandy).

Shopping

Gifts include embroidery and lace, handpainted pottery and porcelain, jewellery, wood carvings and other craft objects. There is a wide variety of fine crystal glass. Have a good look around in the pretty shops and boutiques of the Old Quarter to find craft products and all kinds of souvenirs.

PRACTICAL INFORMATION

Banks. Generally open Monday–Friday 8 a.m.–5 p.m. Money and travellers cheques can also be changed in bureaux de change, larger hotels, many shops and in post offices. The import and export of Slovak currency is prohibited.

Credit cards, travellers cheques. Internationally recognized credit cards and travellers cheques are accepted as payment in larger hotels, restaurants and shops.

Currency. The currency is the Slovak crown (*Slovenská koruna*, abbreviated Sk). One crown = 100 heller (*halér*, plural *halierov*). Coins: 10 heller to 10 crowns. Notes: 20 to 5000 crowns.

Language. The official language is Slovakian. Czech, Hungarian, English and German are also spoken.

Post offices. Monday–Friday 8 a.m.–6 p.m.

Shops. Usually open Monday–Friday 9 a.m.–6 or 7 p.m. and Saturday 9 a.m.–noon. Some shops also open on Sunday mornings. Smaller shops close for lunch noon–2 p.m.

Transport. Buses and trams mostly operate 4.30 a.m.–midnight. Taxis are cheap.

BUDAPEST

Paris of the East

The city of Budapest conjures up a string of flattering adjectives: dramatic, enchanting, glamorous, magical. It's difficult to decide from which angle the "Paris of the East" is most breathtaking: looking over the majestic river towards the monumental expanse of Pest from the heights of Buda, or rather in the direction of the hills and towers of Buda from Pest down below.

The mighty Danube, second-longest river in Europe, flows through the heart of Hungary's capital, and is as essential to its fascination as the Thames is to London or the Seine to Paris. Long, elegant boulevards and stately buildings enhance the Parisian atmosphere, as do the romantic riverside walkways and the general air of pleasure in the good things in life. One of those good things is a soak in a thermal bath, for Budapest is a highly reputed health resort.

Buda, the old town of Obuda, and Pest were separate entities until 1849, when the first permanent bridge was built over the Danube. They did not legally become one until 1873, and even now the city's component parts fit together like pieces of a mismatched jigsaw puzzle. Buda's hills, reaching almost to the river, represent the last ripples of the Transdanubian mountains, while Pest stands on the very edge of the awesomely flat Great Plain.

Politics and geography contrived to make Budapest the main point of contact between Eastern and Western Europe, and popular with tourists from both sides of the postwar ideological divide. The city was the show window for a "goulash communism" that made Hungary the envy of Soviet bloc consumers. The red stars have now disappeared and those days are forgotten; Budapest is now resolutely Western-looking and seems to be on *everyone's* travel agenda.

Budapest was devastated by World War II, and some of its buildings still bear the scars of conflict. But thanks to inspired restoration, the city has recovered most of its former glory. With its venerable buildings, splendid panoramas, quaint medieval streets and museums of every kind, it's an exciting place to visit. When you feel tired, pause for a relaxing wallow in one of the city's many Turkish baths. At night, what could be more romantic than dining to the sound of gypsy violins as you watch the lights play on the Danube—without question Budapest's trump card.

A BRIEF HISTORY

3rd century BC– 14th century AD

Celts build a stronghold on Buda's Gellért Hill dominating the Danube. The region is on the Roman Empire's main line of defence against the barbarians. When Rome weakens, Attila the Hun reigns here until his death in 453. Magyar tribes migrate across the Carpathian mountains to the central Hungarian plain in 896. The first king, Stephen I, oversees the conversion of his people to Christianity. After a Mongol invasion in the 13th century, King Béla IV revives the nation, building a number of fortified towns. The Árpád dynasty dies out in 1301, and foreign kings rule.

15th–18th centuries

A Turkish invasion is repelled in 1456. The victor's son, Matthias Corvinus, rules during Hungary's Golden Age (1458–1490). The Turks return in 1526, and this time they stay for 150 years. When they are finally routed in 1686, Hungary becomes part of the Austrian Empire. An unsuccessful war for independence rages from 1703 to 1711. Despite political dissatisfaction, the country makes great economic strides under the Austrian regime.

19th century

Another revolt, in 1848–49, is crushed by the combined forces of Austria and Russia. In 1867 the Dual Monarchy is established. The cities of Pest, Buda and Obuda merge in 1873 to form Budapest, the capital.

20th century

As part of the Austro-Hungarian Empire, Hungary supports Germany during World War I, with disastrous results. World War II is equally catastrophic: the country is occupied by Hitler's troops in 1944, and when Budapest finally falls to the Soviets a year later, only one in four of the city's buildings is still intact. Hungary becomes a Soviet satellite, and undergoes sweeping nationalization. The uprising of 1956 leads to a new administration, under János Kádár, aimed at improving economic conditions and relaxing political severities. In 1989's whirlwind of ideological changes, Hungary tears apart the Iron Curtain and turns to democratic government and a free economy. The country will become part of the EU in 2004.

Sightseeing

As with any great city, Budapest has far too many attractions to cover in a short time. If you can, it is ideal to wander round at leisure and get to know the city by degrees. The best place to start is in Buda.

The Castle District

This fascinating zone of cobbled streets, hidden gardens and medieval courtyards hovers over the rest of Budapest on a long, narrow plateau. Towering gracefully above the old town is the neo-Gothic spire of the **Matthias Church**. Founded in the 13th century by King Béla IV, it has witnessed many dramatic events: the excommunication of a Pope, the splendid wedding of Matthias Corvinus to Beatrice of Aragon and the coronation in 1867 of the Austrian Emperor Franz Joseph as King of Hungary. The building itself is essentially 19th-century neo-Gothic, attached to what the Turks left of the original edifice in 1686. The **Loreto Chapel** contains the revered statue of the Virgin once buried by the Turks in the chapel walls. It is said to have reappeared miraculously during the siege of 1686.

Nearby rises an undulating white rampart with gargoyles and cloisters: the **Fishermen's Bastion**. Built on the site of a medieval fish market, it recalls the fact that in the 18th century local fishermen were responsible for defending the fortifications. The present Disneyesque structure dates from early in the 20th century. The arches frame the river artistically, as if they had been designed especially for photographers.

Looking west, you face the tinted glass façade of the **Hilton Hotel**. The building incorporates the remains of a 17th-century Jesuit college and a 13th-century abbey. In the lobby is an ancient milestone, found on the site, which once marked the limit of the Roman Empire.

The Castle District is only four streets wide and easily covered on foot. As you walk around, it is worth peeking into the big doorways to discover otherwise hidden architectural details, such as sculpted stone seats. In 1800 Beethoven stayed in the baroque mansion at No. 7 Táncsics Mihály utca. This was the Jewish quarter until the 16th century; the house now contains the Museum of Music History.

The main road, Országház utca, was once called the street of baths. Many medieval features remain. At No. 2, a restaurant occupies a grand 15th-century mansion with a cloistered courtyard. The street leads into

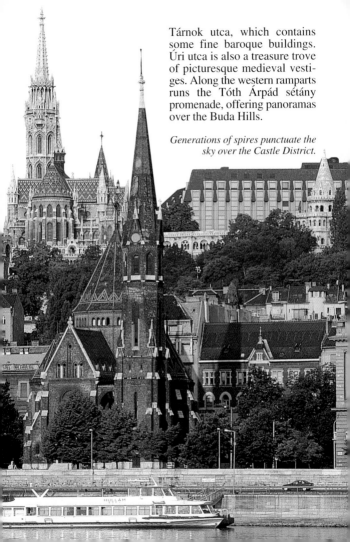

Tárnok utca, which contains some fine baroque buildings. Úri utca is also a treasure trove of picturesque medieval vestiges. Along the western ramparts runs the Tóth Árpád sétány promenade, offering panoramas over the Buda Hills.

Generations of spires punctuate the sky over the Castle District.

The Royal Palace

After a long and turbulent history, including complete destruction after World War II, the palace begun in the 13th century by Béla IV was restored to its former splendour and offers a delightful view over Pest and the Danube from its walls. The building houses three excellent museums. In the baroque south wing, the **History Museum** evokes the city's evolution since the Bronze Age. Downstairs in the excavated part of the medieval castle you can see a roomful of striking Gothic statues unearthed in 1974. The **Hungarian National Gallery**, an impressive modern exhibition of Hungarian art from the Middle Ages to the present day, occupies the centre under the dome. You enter from the terrace overlooking the Danube.

The **Museum of Contemporary Art** (Ludwig Collection) puts on temporary exhibitions, while its huge collection is rotated regularly, so you can never be sure whether you will see works by Picasso, Baselit, Lichtenstein, Warhol or Hungarian artists such as Endre Tót, Molnár and Erdély.

Danube Views

Gellért Hill, right alongside the Danube, takes its name from an Italian missionary (Gerard) who converted the Hungarians but was eventually thrown from the hill in a barrel spiked with nails, in 1046, by militant heathens. The summit is dominated by the severe-looking **Citadel**. Built in the mid-19th century, it served in World War II as the last stronghold of the German occupying army. A conspicuous modern addition to the hilltop is the **Liberation Monument**, visible from many parts of the city. While most Soviet-inspired statuary was transferred to Szoborpark, on the city outskirts, after the collapse of communism, the gigantic woman brandishing a palm frond was considered too important a part of the skyline to jettison.

Down below, riverside Buda is known as Watertown because of its thermal baths. **Rudas Baths**, one of the most colourful, has been in business since 1556.

At the Buda side of the Chain Bridge (Szechenyi Lánchid), a **funicular** reaches Castle Hill just north of the Royal Palace gates. It provides one of the most scenic rides in Budapest, and has been in operation since 1870. A short walk north of the Chain Bridge, in Batthyány tér, the twin-towered **St Anne's Church** is one of the most striking baroque structures in the city. Designed by a Jesuit,

Ignatius Pretelli, in Italian style in the mid-18th century, the interior is a dazzling drama of huge statues and black marble columns.

Continuing from the square up Fő utca, you reach another 16th-century Turkish bath, the **Király Gyógyfürdő**, with a stone dome and octagonal pool. Further along is the **Gül Baba Türbéje**, still another relic of the Turkish era. The meticulously preserved tomb was built over the grave of a renowned dervish.

Óbuda

North of Buda, surrounded by concrete highrises, busy roads and flyovers, are the remains of **Aquincum**, which developed from legionnaires' camp to the Roman capital of Lower Pannonia.

There's an amphitheatre on the corner of Nagyszombat utca and Pacsirtamező út, and military baths near the Árpád híd train station, but they have not been well maintained. The calmest spot in which to dwell on the Roman past is at the **Aquincum Museum**, built on the site of the main civil town. It displays excavated items and a model of what the town would have looked like.

Afterwards, explore the cobbled squares of central Óbuda, enlivened by cafés, restaurants and galleries. In a fine old mansion on Szentlélek tér, next to the Árpad Híd station, the **Vasarely Museum** displays more than 350 works of the Op Art pioneer.

Margaret Island

When the Romans were exhausted by the wear and tear of life in Aquincum, *Margit sziget* is where they came to rest. Comprising mostly parkland, woods and gardens, Margaret Island is an almost traffic-free haven of beauty and peace in the middle of the Danube. Probably like the Romans, today's visitors put the accent on culture both physical and cerebral, enjoying a sporting complex, thermal baths and an open-air theatre. Near the theatre, wander through the ruins of the 13th-century **Dominican convent** founded by Béla IV, where his daughter Margaret spent most of her life.

Pest

Across the river there are no hills to climb, but the busy streets and imposing boulevards offer plenty to see. The oldest surviving structure in Pest, nestled against the flyover leading to Elizabeth Bridge, is the **Inner City Parish Church**. Founded in the 12th century, it served 63

CENTRAL BUDAPEST

1 Császár Bath
2 Lukács Baths
3 Gül Baba Tomb
4 Zoo
5 Széchenyi Baths
6 Museum of Fine Arts
7 Art Gallery
8 Castle of Vajdahunyad
9 Transport Museum
10 Iron Foundry Museum
11 Király Baths
12 Western Railway Station
13 Ethnographic Museum
14 Parliament
15 Museum of East Asian Art
16 Museum of Chinese Art
17 St Anne's Church
18 State Opera House
19 St Stephen's Basilica
20 Eastern Railway Station
21 Underground Railway Museum
22 Lutheran Museum
23 Jewish Religious and Historical
   Museum
24 City Hall
25 Post Office
26 Semmelweis Museum
27 Inner City Parish Church
28 Franciscan Church
29 University
30 Hungarian National Museum
31 University Church
32 St Gellért Monument
33 Rudas Baths
34 Citadel
35 Statue of Liberty
36 Central Market
37 Applied Arts Museum

some time as a mosque under the Turkish occupation, and a Muslim prayer niche is still to be seen near the altar. In the adjacent square, Március 15. tér, a sunken park displays the excavations of the Roman outpost **Contra-Aquincum**.

The cobbled centrepiece of an expansive pedestrian zone, **Váci utca** is packed with shops selling local wine and food, art and antiques, cosmetics, fashion and jewellery. Street vendors hawk all manner of goods. There are several cafés and restaurants where you can sit back and contemplate the street's eclectic architectural mix, up above the shopfronts.

Towards the Chain Bridge at **Martinelli tér**, stand back and admire the square's Art Nouveau architecture.

Vestiges of the city's medieval walls have been attractively incorporated into more recent buildings, notably in the streets that form part of the **Kiskörút** boulevard, bending its way from the Szabadság Bridge to Deák tér, and changing names along the way. One of its most fascinating landmarks is at 1 Vámház körút, a cavernous red-brick and cast-iron **covered market**, full of local colour and exotic smells. It opened in 1897. The ground floor is crammed with food stalls selling every

conceivable ingredient for a gourmet Hungarian meal, while upstairs are as many souvenir and novelty stalls as you could ever want in one place.

The Múzeum körút section is dominated by the **Hungarian National Museum**, with a magnificent neoclassical façade. The huge exhibition is imaginatively designed and covers the entire drama of the nation's history, from the settlement of the Magyars in the Carpathian Basin to the collapse of communism and advent of democracy more than a thousand years later. The highlight is the beautiful Hungarian crown jewels, displayed separately in their own darkened room. The cross on the top of the crown was bent when the jewels were smuggled out of the country to escape the Mongols. They eventually found their way to Fort Knox and were restored to Hungary only in 1978.

Vámház körút and Múzeum körút intersect at Kálvin tér, where you might wish to make a foray into Üllői út to visit the building truly pulsating with shocks that houses the **Museum of Applied Arts**. The style of the brick-and-ceramic-tile palace is listed as Art Nouveau, though it might be better described as Fantasy Hungarian with strong eastern influences.

The exhibits tell a terse history of ceramics in China, Europe and, in particular, Hungary. Also on show are furniture, textiles, oriental rugs, metalwork, clocks and curios made by extremely talented Hungarian and foreign hands.

On Dohány utca you will see the twin onion-domed towers of the Central Synagogue, the biggest in Europe and built in a strange oriental-Byzantine style. Within the complex is the **Jewish Museum**, reflecting many centuries of Jewish life in Hungary. It houses some spine-chilling documents on the fate of the Budapest ghetto in World War II.

At the Deák tér end of the boulevard, the **Metro Museum,** inside the station, recounts the building of the Millennial Railway.

Continuing on from Deák tér is Bajcsy-Zsilinszky út, one of the boulevards that give the city its Parisian air. On the west side towers the city's largest church, **St Stephen's Basilica**. Under construction from 1851–1905, it was worked on by three successive architects, in as many different styles. Its most revered relic is the mummified right hand of St Stephen, kept in a silver reliquary. You can climb the dome for a splendid view over the rooftops.

To the northwest along the embankment, the **Houses of Parliament** symbolize the grandeur of the Austro-Hungarian Empire, looking much like their British counterpart.

Be sure to take a stroll along the most stately avenue in Budapest, **Andrássy út**, modelled after the Champs-Elysées in the 1870s. Its name has been changed many times, but by any title this remains a spacious, patrician thoroughfare. Stop in at the **Postal Museum** at No. 3, which has a surprisingly entertaining collection of curiosities.

The neo-Renaissance **State Opera House** is the most admired building on the avenue. Statues of 16 great composers stand high above the entrance, with Franz Liszt and Ferenc Erkel in places of honour.

At no. 103, the **Ferenc Hopp Museum of Asiatic Art** displays splendid collections of Chinese Buddhist sculptures, Indian paintings, Japanese silks and so on, amassed by a wealthy businessman.

The avenue ends with a flourish at the vast and airy **Heroes' Square**, with the Millenary Monument as its centrepiece, topped by statue of the Archangel Gabriel. Begun on the thousandth anniversary of the Magyar conquest, the monument depicts Prince Árpád and his chieftains enclosed in a colonnade of Hungary's most illustrious leaders, ranging from King Stephen I to Kossuth, the 1848 revolutionary.

Facing each other across the expanse of Heroes' Square are two almost identical neoclassical buildings. The larger one is the **Museum of Fine Arts**, whose comprehensive collection of paintings, including a number of French Impressionists, makes it an institution of international importance. The smaller clone, the **Art Gallery**, houses temporary exhibitions of paintings by Hungarian and foreign artists.

Beyond the Millenary Monument sprawls the vast **City Park**. Among its amenities is an artificial lake and the extraordinary Castle of Vajdahunyad, modelled on a Transylvanian castle. In front sits the hooded statue of a royal scribe known only as Anonymous, who wrote the first Hungarian chronicles. The figure of George Washington was presented to Budapest in 1906 by Hungarian settlers in the United States.

East of the castle, **Petőfi Hall** has an arena for rock concerts and discos, a Museum of Aviation and Space Travel, and a weekend flea market.

Across from the park rises the triple dome of the **Széchenyi Baths**, one of Europe's largest medicinal bath complexes. The amusing sight of people industriously playing chess while soaking in the healing waters is not to be missed.

Excursions

Some 30 km (18 miles) south of Budapest, the town of **Gödöllö** is particularly known for its castle. In 1867, when the emperor Franz Joseph I of Austria and his wife Elisabeth (Sissi) were crowned King and Queen of Hungary, they received the castle as a wedding gift.

The royal pair's regular visits gave the region a new significance. The empress came often, delighted to escape from the stiff etiquette of Vienna and to practise her favourite sport, horse riding. The castle, built from 1744 to 1748 by Andreas Mayerhoffer, was renovated in 1997. Tours include the state rooms, the park and the stables.

Puszta

Also known as the Great Plain (Nagyalföld), this vast, flat prairie was Hungary's very own Wild West during the 19th century, when huge herds of cattle grazed here watched over by cowboys, called *gulyás*. It was once covered in thick forest, but was laid waste during the Turkish occupation, because of the invaders' need for timber to build fortresses, and became a virtual desert. Its renaissance as pastureland was due to the irrigation works on the River Tisza employed by Count Széchenyi in the early 19th century. But by the 20th century, the success of the irrigation scheme meant it could sustain crop development, and big landowners carried out wholesale enclosure, killing off the cattle industry and creating widespread poverty among the peasants. Under post-war communism, the estates were nationalized, and huge collective farms introduced, only to be broken up after 1989 and returned to private ownership.

Today, you will find pleasant little towns—Kecskemét and Szeged in particular are worth spending time in—beyond which are attractive old white-washed farmsteads adorned with bright-coloured strings of paprika. The plains, meanwhile, are as strong on atmosphere as ever.

Lake Balaton

Balaton is one of the largest lakes in Europe. It is strikingly elongated, stretching for 77 km (48 miles) along the foothills of the Bakony Mountains, but only 14 km (8.7 miles) across at its widest point. It is also remarkably shallow—a mere 11 m (36 ft) at its maximum depth. This has some interesting side effects. It freezes over completely in winter, making it one of the world's great skating rinks, while in summer the water heats up like a thermal bath. Its shallowness also makes it vulnerable to strong winds, which can create high waves in a matter of minutes.

The lakewater is packed with minerals which, given the Hungarian love of spas, means there are a number of health resorts. Balatonfüred, on the northeast shore, has been frequented for its medicinal springs for the last 250 years.

Dining Out

A popular appetizer is *libamáj-pástétom*, flaky pastry filled with goose-liver pâté. *Hortobágyi húsos palacsinta* are pancakes filled with minced meat and sour cream; *gombafejek rántva*, breadcrumb-coated fried mushrooms. Now for the goulash, which is not at all a spicy stew, but a thinnish soup. Called *gulyásleves*, it combines bits of beef, vegetables, caraway seeds and paprika for colour and zing. *Szegedi halászlé* is a freshwater fish soup. On a hot day, cold fruit soups *(hidegyümölcsleves)*, made from cherries or apricots, are very refreshing.

For the fish course, try *paprikás ponty*, carp with a paprika sauce; *rácponty*, carp stew with sour cream; or *pisztráng tejszín mártásbán*, baked trout with cream.

Hungarians are extremely fond of large helpings of meat. *Pörkölt* or *bográcsgulyás* is the spicy stew that non-Hungarians mistakenly call "goulash". On many menus you'll see *paprikás csirke*, chicken with sour cream and paprika. *Töltött paprika* are stuffed peppers; *bélszin Budapest módra* is a thick beef steak served "à la Budapest" with a sauce of peppers, mushrooms, peas and chopped chicken livers.

The Hungarians excel in the dessert department, so be sure to save some room for a strudel *(rétes)* filled with *almás* (apple), *mákos* (poppy seeds), *meggyes* (sour cherries) or *túrós* (lemon, raisins and cottage cheese); or *Gundel palacsinta*, pancakes with a rich filling of chopped walnuts and raisins, covered in chocolate sauce and flambéed with brandy or rum. For more simple tastes, there is always ice cream *(fagylalt)* or fruit *(gyümölcs)*.

Shopping

Budapest's fanciest shops are concentrated on Váci utca, a pedestrian mall, and its side streets.

For starters, tourists will surely want to return home with some of the world-famous hand-painted Herend porcelain, ranging from a tiny flower-patterned brooch or an adorable little snail with gilded shell to a full dinner service. Here are some other good buys.

Handicrafts: articles of copper, brass or fine silver; rustic hand-carved wood articles; leather goods.

Textiles: handmade carpets and rugs in traditional patterns; peasant-style embroidered shirts and blouses; finely embroidered linenware.

Food and drink: cotton or paper sachets of ground paprika (in varying strengths); spicy dried sausage; a garland of dried cherry peppers; packaged cake or strudel; a bottle of wine or fruit brandy. Finally, CDs and tapes: Liszt, Kodály and Bartók in a variety of recordings; folk music and gypsy violins.

PRACTICAL INFORMATION

Climate. The city can become very hot and humid, especially in July and August when many town dwellers head for the cooler shores of Lake Balaton. Winters are cold. The best weather is in May and September, when Budapest is pleasantly mild and fairly crowd-free.

Currency. The *forint* (Ft.) is issued in coins from 1 to 100 Ft. and banknotes from 200 to 20,000 Ft. Retain all currency exchange receipts to re-exchange forints when leaving the country. Do not change money on the street. Many tourist-oriented establishments accept international credit cards, and US dollars are accepted even on market stalls.

Driving. Budapest is difficult to navigate as there are no left turns, and the roads are not in perfect condition, with on-going repairs everywhere. Better take a taxi, and try to agree on a fare before you set off.

Opening hours. *Banks* are generally open Monday to Friday 9 a.m–2 p.m., until noon on Saturdays. *Post offices*, Monday to Friday 8 a.m.–6 p.m. Saturdays to 2 p.m.; the main post office and those in the east and west railway stations are open round the clock. *Shops* are usually open 10 a.m.–6 p.m. (Thursdays to 8 p.m.); food shops as early as 6 or 7 a.m.

Safety. Although crime levels have risen since the fall of communism, Budapest remains a fairly safe city by Western standards. It is nonetheless worth taking some basic precautions. Only carry the money you will need for the day along with a credit card. Watch out for pickpockets in tourist areas and on public transport, and beware of scams aimed at foreigners along Váci utca, which will end up with you and your money parting company.

Sales tax. A tax of 16 per cent is imposed on goods in Hungary. To benefit from a tax refund, your purchase in any one store must amount to a minimum of 50,000 Ft. Ask the sales assistant for a fiscal invoice, a VAT Reclaim form and a tax-free envelope. Keep all receipts for currency exchange and your credit card slips, and when you leave the country, have all these documents stamped by a Hungarian Customs Officer. Shops offering this service display a Tax-Free Shopping logo.

Tipping. Waiters and taxi drivers expect a tip of 10–15 per cent.

Transport. The Budapest Transport Company (BKV) runs a large network of buses, trams and trolleybuses as well as three metro lines and, in summer, a ferry service on the Danube. The system is efficient, reliable, good value and gets you within walking distance of just about all the main sights. Most public transport starts at around 4.30 a.m. and goes on till 11.30 p.m. Maps of the system can be bought at the main metro and railway stations.

INDEX

General Editor
Barbara Ender-Jones
Photo Credits
Frédérique Fasser: pp. 3, 20, 27, 38, 41;
Renata Holzbachová: p. 43;
Österreichische Galerie Belvedere Wien (detail): p 46;
Marguerite Martinoli: pp. 55, 70;
Hémisphères/Wysocki: p. 61
Maps
Huber Kartographie;
JPM Publications

Printed in Switzerland
Weber/Bienne (CTP) — 03/03/01